# The Lonely Queue

The forgotten history of the courageous
Chinese Americans in Los Angeles

勇敢的洛杉磯華人所留下的一段被遺忘的歷史

By Icy Smith
Chinese Translation by Emily Wang

鄧瑞冰　著

王國蘭　中文譯述

**East** **West** Discovery Press

Published by East West Discovery Press
Author: Icy Smith
Chinese Translation: Emily Wang
Design and Production: Albert Lin
Photography Research: Icy Smith

Publisher's Cataloging-in-Publication
(Provided by Quality Books, Inc.)

Smith, Icy.
    The lonely queue: the forgotten history of the courageous Chinese Americans in Los Angeles/by Icy Smith ; Chinese translation by Emily Wang. – 2nd ed.
        p. cm.
    Includes bibliographical references.
    LCCN: 2001118112
    ISBN: 0-9701654-1-2

    Chinese Americans—California—Los Angeles— History. 2. Chinese Americans—California—Los Angeles—Social conditions—History. 3. Chinese Americans—California—Los Angeles—Economic conditions-History.    I. Title.

F869.L89C5 2000            305.8951'079494
                                QBI00-500062


ISBN: 0-9701654-1-2
LCCN: 2001118112


Printed in Hong Kong, Published in the United States of America
Published in 2001.

# The Lonely Queue

The forgotten history of the courageous
Chinese Americans in Los Angeles

Foreword by
Chinese Historical Society of Southern California

# *Foreword*

*In the recent past, scholarly research by individuals such as Paul de Falla, William M. Mason, Raymond Lou, Roberta Greenwood and Harry Lawton, has documented various aspects of the history of the local Chinese American community. Other works, by journalists and lay writers, have appeared in newspapers and popular media.*

*Now, in The Lonely Queue, independent writer Icy Smith has written a volume for the popular market, with a perspective on the entire development of the Southern California Chinese American community. This pictorial book features more than 200 photographs from a number of public archives and private collections. She chronicles the community's struggles and triumphs during the past 150 years, conveying the indomitable spirit of the early immigrants, and recognizing the workers, entrepreneurs, and leaders for their roles in the development of the Los Angeles area.*

*Books such as The Lonely Queue are very important in advancing cultural understanding. Here is an example as to why: The Southern California city of Monterey Park drew national attention in 1985 when controversy and conflict arose around the issue of Chinese language signs on numerous businesses in that community. At the City Council meeting, some residents demanded that the city require that all signs in the community contain English only. In rebuttal, one Chinese American in the audience stood up and pointed out that since many of the local street names used the Spanish language, and others with Italian, German and French, it would be as expensive as it would be ridiculous to implement such a demand. To further his point he asked the audience, didn't the word 'America' come from an Italian name? And since Chinese Americans have played a vital role in the development of Southern California, beginning from California statehood in 1850, how long does it take to become part of America?*

*The controversy in Monterey Park was made more acute because by the 1980 census Asian Americans already outnumbered the white population in Monterey Park. That census also showed that Los Angeles County had more persons of Chinese ethnicity than any other county in the nation; Los Angeles International Airport had replaced Ellis Island and Angel Island as one of the leading ports of entry for Asian immigrants. With these changes, conflict and misunderstandings arose, in part due to misperceptions about the new immigrant community, and in part due to a lack of knowledge of the vital role that Chinese Americans have played in Southern California history.*

*The Chinese Historical Society of Southern California applauds the efforts of Icy Smith and others who made this book possible. We hope it will inspire further study in the history of Chinese Americans. But more importantly, it is hoped that this work will help people of all ages and colors to better understand the Chinese American community, past and present, and to recognize that Chinese Americans have long been a part of America.*

*Chinese Historical Society of Southern California*

*To contact the Society:*

*Call: (323) 222-1918*

*Write: PO Box 862647, Los Angeles, CA 90086-2647*

*E-mail: chssc@hotmail.com*

# 代　序

近年來，有些學者對地方美籍華人社區史的不同層面進行考証，如Paul de Falla, William M. Mason, Raymond Lou, Roberta Greenwood and Harry Lawton。其他由記者與業餘作家撰述的文獻也在報章及大傳媒體上刊載流傳。

獨立作家鄧瑞冰(Icy Smith)撰寫的新作《寂寞的辮子》(The Lonely Queue)記載了南加州華人社區的發展。該書收錄近二百幅館藏與私人收藏的圖片。作者敘述了一百五十年來華人經歷的奮鬥與勝利，展現了華裔先民不屈不撓的精神，寫下華工、企業家，以及社區領袖在洛杉磯地區發展中的貢獻。

如同《寂寞的辮子》的書籍對於促進不同文化之間的了解至關重要，以下即為一例，一九八五年，南加州蒙特利公園市的商招獨尊英語一事受到全國矚目，當時，許多商號使用中文商招而導致社區廣泛爭議與衝突，在市議會上，一些居民要求市府規定社區所有商招只可使用英文，在場一位華人起而反駁道，既然許多本地街名使用了西班牙文，還有一些使用意大利文、德文，以及法文，要求商招統一使用英文的規定既荒謬又耗費資金。為了進一步闡述他的觀點，他問在場人士，「難道'America'一詞不是源於一個意大利名嗎？」自一八五零年加州成立起，美籍華人在南加州的發展中扮演極重要的角色，但華人還要多久才能真正為美國社會所接受。

根據一九八零年人口統計，蒙特利公園市的亞裔美人人口已經超過白人人口總數，這場爭議更形尖銳。報告中還指出，洛杉磯華裔人數為全美各縣之冠，洛杉磯國際機場也已取代伊利斯島(Ellis Island)與天使島(Angel Island)，而名列亞洲移民入關港口之首，衝突與誤解卻也隨之而起，部分原因是出於對新移民社區的誤解，而另一方面則在於對華裔美人對南加歷史之重大貢獻欠缺了解。

南加華人歷史學會慶賀鄧瑞冰女士完成本書的成就，並向協力完成本書的其他人士致意。我們期盼本書將激勵各界對華裔歷史的進一步研究，更希望本書將有助於所有讀者更深入了解今昔的華裔社區，並肯定華裔早已是美國的一部分。

南加州華人歷史學會

與本學會聯繫：

Tel:(323)222-1918

PO Box 862647, Los Angeles, CA 90086-2647

E-mail:  chssc@hotmail.com

# Acknowledgments

*I am grateful to the Chinese Historical Society of Southern California which contributed greatly to the formation of this book. They have continuously documented the history of the local Chinese-American community through numerous essays and books such as "Origins and Destinations", "Linking Our Lives", and "Duty and Honor".*

*I am also indebted to the generations of scholars who have written extensive Chinese-American history, and especially the following people for giving me invaluable advice on the book's content and making it a better book: Suellen Cheng, Gilbert Hom, Munson Kwok, Margie Lew, Eugene Moy, Jean Bruce Poole, Ella Quan, Michael Smith, and Johnny Yee. Special thanks also go to Jennifer Knight for her editing effort, Professor Gillian Dale, Eugene Moy and Gilbert Hom for their proofreading assistance, and James Kuo for his production advice. I also owe my greatest thanks to my associates Emily Wang for translating the text into Chinese, and Albert Lin for producing this spectacular book. Their endless support is very much appreciated.*

*I would like to thank Jim Fong, Roger Hong, Howard Jong, Gilbert Hom, David and Yuki Lee, Mei Ong, Wallace Quon, Delbert and Dolores Wong, Wilbur Woo, Johnny Yee and Nancy Yee who generously shared their vintage photographs as I cherished the opportunity to learn about their inspiring experiences. Special thanks also go to Suellen Cheng of the Chinese Historical Society of Southern California, El Pueblo de Los Angeles Historical Monument, Chinese American Museum, John Cahoon of the Seaver Center for Western History Research, Natural History Museum of Los Angeles County, Carolyn Cole of the Los Angeles Public Library, Dace Taube of the USC Regional History Center, Carlos Figueroa of the Community Redevelopment Agency, William Chun Hoon and Carol Duan of the Friends of the Chinatown Library, and Steve Comba of the Montgomery Gallery of Pomona College for their special efforts on my photography research.*

*Also, I would like to thank the Natural History Museum of Los Angeles County as an in-kind donor, and the Chinese Chamber of Commerce of Los Angeles as the initial major sponsor for this book. Last but not least, I would like to thank my husband Michael for giving me intellectual guidance and support on this project.*

*Responses to this book:*

*Though the material in the book has been carefully researched, factual mistakes can be made. I would appreciate comments, corrections and feedback. I welcome contributions of additional stories and photographs of Chinese Americans in Southern California so that they may possibly be incorporated in a second edition of this book. You may contact me by writing to the East West Discovery Press, P.O. Box 2393, Gardena, CA 90247.*

# 感　謝

本人對南加州華人歷史學會協助本書的完成與出版，在此深致謝意，學會長時間以來，爲文著述如"Origins and Destinations "、" Linking Our Live "、" Duty and Honor "，爲本地的華裔社區留下了歷史記錄。

而曾經詳細記錄華裔史蹟的前輩學者們，也令我受益良多，特別是以下數位人士針對本書內容所給我的寶貴意見，令本書更爲周延詳實，Suellen Cheng、Gilbert Hom、Munson Kwok、Margie Lew、Eugene Moy、Jean Bruce Poole、Ella Quan、Michael Smith, 與 Johnny Yee。同時還要特別感謝Gillian Dale教授, Eugene Moy和 Gilbert Hom 的協助校稿，James Kuo 的印刷諮詢，Jennifer Knight爲編輯本書所做的努力，更要向和我一起努力的夥伴：中文譯述Emily Wang，美編設計Albert Lin，致最深的謝意。

同時，我要感謝Jim Fong、Roger Hong、Gilbert Hom、David and Yuki Lee、Mei Ong、Wallace Quon、Delbert and Dolores Wong、Wilbur Woo、Johnny Yee 和 Nancy Yee，他們慷慨地提供珍藏的相片，讓我有幸能與讀者分享他們豐富的人生經歷。於此並向協助我進行圖片考証的南加州華人歷史學會的Suellen Cheng、洛杉磯縣歷史博物館西方歷史研究Seaver中心的John Cahoon、洛杉磯圖書館的Carolyn Cole、南加大地區歷史中心的Dacc Taube、社區重建局的Carlos Figueroa、華埠圖書館之友的William Chun Hoon 和 Carol Duan，及波莫那學院蒙哥瑪利畫廊的Steve Comba 等，一併致謝。

此外，我也要感激羅省中華總商會率先贊助本書編印，最後，我更要感謝外子給我的指導與支持。

本書所載的所有資料雖經仔細研究考証，恐仍有疏忽錯誤，懇請各界不吝指正，並敬邀南加華裔爲本書二版繼續提供相關的故事與圖片。

來函請寄： East West Discovery Press， P.O. Box 2393, Gardena, CA 90247.

寂寞的辮子

The Lonely Queue

# Table of Contents
目錄

寂寞的辮子

# Los Angeles
# Old Chinatown Map,
# circa 1920

Courtesy of El Pueblo de Los Angeles
Historical Monument, Chinese American
Museum Collection.

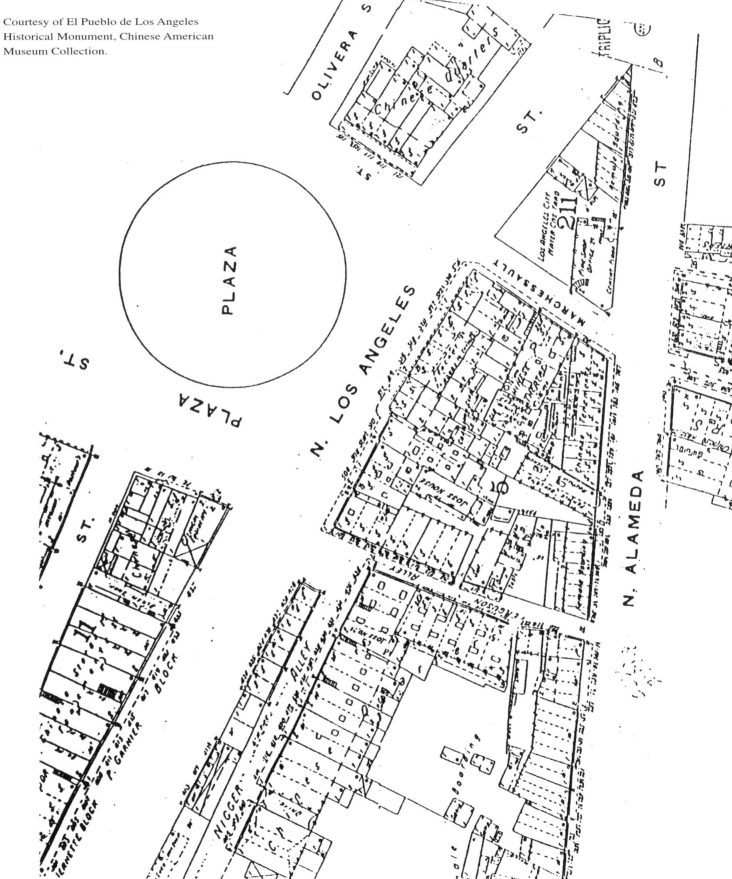

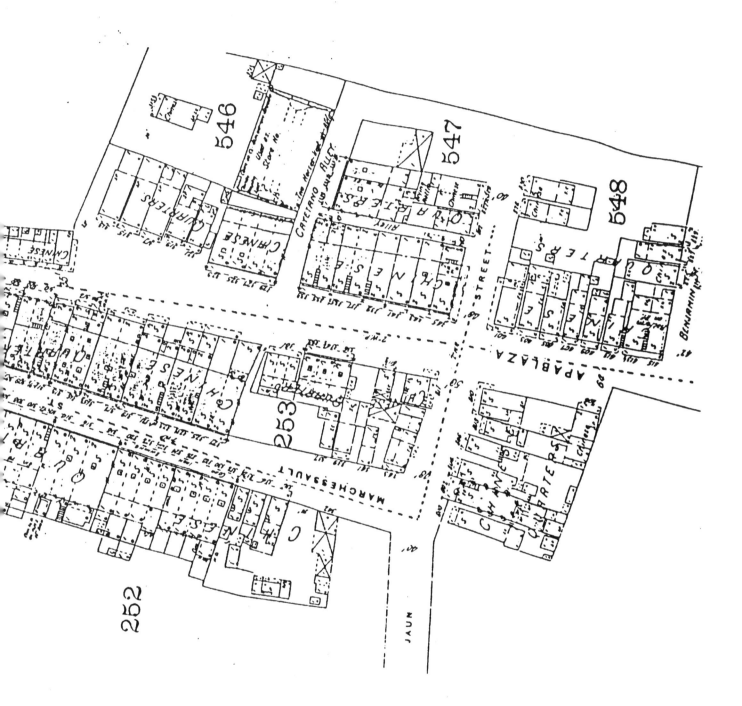

N

# *Chapter 1*

*Early Settlement in Los Angeles*
洛衫磯早期移民

### 1850-1885  Early Settlement

The first permanent Chinese settlement in Los Angeles started with three men in 1856.[1] But, only two Chinese male house servants, Ah Fou and Ah Luce, were recorded in the 1850 United States Census. By 1860, the census showed a total of 15 Chinese men and two women.[2]

### 1850-1885  早期移民

一八五六年時，第一批華裔永久居民僅有三名男子。[1] 而一八五零年的全美人口普查只登錄著兩名自稱是阿福和阿祿的男僕。一八六零年時的人口普查則記載有十五名華裔男子和兩名女子。[2]

Chinese and black miners on a railroad hand car in Auburn. Anti-Chinese sentiment intensified as the number of Chinese miners increased between 1850 - 1854. They were physically expelled from one mining camp after another.

華人和黑人礦工在Auburn的鐵路平板車上。一八五零年至一八五四年間，排華情緒隨華工人數增加而高漲。他們不斷被逐出礦場。

Photo courtesy of Seaver Center for Western History Research, Natural History Museum of Los Angeles County

Three white and four Chinese gold miners working beside a sluice box in the Auburn Ravine in 1851.

一八五一年，三名白人和四名華人礦工在Auburn Ravine的洗礦槽旁。

Photo courtesy of Seaver Center for Western History Research, Natural History Museum of Los Angeles County

Beginning in 1864, Chinese laborers were brought in from mainland China to build the Central Pacific Railroad – the western half of the country's first transcontinental railroad. Laborers used hand tools such as picks, shovels, axes and black blasting powder.

一八六四年，來自中國大陸的華工修築中央太平洋鐵路—美國第一條橫跨美洲大陸鐵路的西半部。華工使用以手操作的原始工具築鐵路，如叉、鏟、鍬和黑炸藥。

Photo courtesy of Seaver Center for Western History Research, Natural History Museum of Los Angeles County

## ▶ Mining

Between 1850 and 1854, Chinese miners accounted for 50 percent of the revenues generated by the California Foreign Miner's Tax and 98 percent of its total from 1854 to 1870. For 20 some years, the Foreign Miner's Tax itself constituted the principal source of revenue for the state. [3] As the number of Chinese miners in the state increased, anti-Chinese sentiment intensified. During the last half of the 1850s, the Chinese were physically expelled from one mining camp after another. Some were robbed and beaten, and some were murdered. These crimes were seldom punished due to the laxity of law enforcement, and a California Supreme Court ruling in 1854 that stated that no Chinese, whether victim or witness, could testify against a white person. The threat of Chinese workers to American labor brought an early issue of hostility between Chinese and whites. As a result, Chinese miners in Northern California may have started to drift into more isolated cities, such as Los Angeles at the time, in search of less dangerous occupations that were not competitive with whites. Many Chinese turned to service industries, such as the laundry or restaurant trade, or entered small-scale manufacturing of such items as brooms and sandals. Even in these occupations, however, the Chinese were not safe from violence. [4]

## 採礦

一八五零至一八五四年間，華裔礦工繳交的所得稅佔加州外籍礦工稅收的百分之五十，一八五四年到一八七零年間，更達百分之九十八。二十多年來外籍礦工稅在當時成為州政府的主要收入來源。[3] 隨著加州華裔礦工人數的增加，反華情緒也隨之高漲。一八五零年代後期，華工硬生生地被逐一趕出各個礦場，有些慘遭搶劫毆打，有些被殺害。由於執法單位的縱容，以及加州最高法院在一八五四年判定不論華人為受害者或證人，均不得出庭指認白人，致使這些罪行甚少受到懲治。華工對本地勞工形成的威脅成為雙方敵對的早期因素，結果使北加地區的華工流落到如洛杉磯等偏遠城市，以避開與白人競爭的局面，尋求危險性較低的職業。許多華人轉而投向服務業，如經營洗衣店和餐館，或是生產掃帚和拖鞋的小工廠。然而，即使在這些行業，華人還是難逃暴力的威迫。[4]

## ▶ Labor

In the early days, some of the Chinese migrating to Los Angeles were miners from northern California who came here to seek their fortunes. California was referred to as "Gum Saan" (Land of the Golden Mountain). Some came here on the credit-ticket system, which allowed Chinese to immigrate to California under the condition that they repay the debt out of their earnings. Others came under the contract-labor system, in which an American company paid for transportation. In return, an immigrant agreed to work for the company for a certain number of years to repay the cost of transportation. Some workers were kidnapped or tricked into signing false contracts, and ended up as slave laborers.[5] However, the Chinese laborers found themselves in a foreign land where they were denied the most basic rights to own property, to testify in court against Caucasians, to intermarry with Caucasians, and to become citizens. The gradual attainment of civil rights took nearly a century.[6]

## 苦力

早期移居洛杉磯的華人中，有些原是北加的礦工遠道來此碰運氣，當時的加州因此又被稱為「金山」。有些華人受華工契約約束，移民來此後，他們要用工資還債；還有些是契約勞工，先由美國公司負擔交通費用，移民則同意在一特定年限內，為該公司工作，用工資償還交通費用。有些工人被脅迫或欺騙，誤簽合同，而成為奴工。[5] 遺憾的是，他們發現自己在這片外國人的土地上並不受歡迎，在充滿敵意的地方，他們不能享有最基本的權利，包括擁有土地的權利、在法庭控訴白人的權利，以及成為公民的權利。華裔為爭取民權，奮戰了近一個世紀。[6]

Chinese men milling around in front of the one-story Chinese-occupied Olvera Adobe located at the corner of Marchessault Street and Los Angeles Street across from the Plaza. A sign on the building advertised "China Merchandise," circa 1880.

一八八零年，馬其索街和洛杉磯街角，The Plaza對街的單層華人土造樓房前，華裔男子正在工作。樓房上的招牌寫著「中國商品」。

Photo courtesy of Seaver Center for Western History Research, Natural History Museum of Los Angeles County

## ▶ Burlingame Treaty

In 1868, the United States and China signed the Burlingame Treaty, which encouraged the flow of Chinese immigrants. With tremendous economic incentives to American merchants and shippers who employed the Chinese immigrants, the Chinese were given the right to immigrate freely to the United States.[7] In the following years, Chinese immigrants took occupations as cooks, laundrymen, gardeners and vegetable growers, jobs considered women's and minority work. Others joined the flourishing fishing camps up and down the coast including some in San Pedro and on Catalina Island. For many years, catching abalone and preparing dried fish proved to be distinct and profitable Chinese enterprises. [8]

## 浦安臣協約

一八六八年，美國與中國簽定浦安臣協約，協約鼓勵華裔移民進入美國，中國同意對垂涎中國市場的美國企業和船公司，給予相當優惠的經濟待遇，美國則給予華人自由移民美國的權利，以此為回報。[7] 往後多年，華裔移民多從事廚子、洗衣工、園丁，和菜農等被認為是女性與少數族裔才會從事的行業。有些華人在聖彼卓和卡塔利納島沿海一帶，捕漁為生。多年來，鮑魚和魚乾已成為高級且利潤又高的華人生意。[8]

In 1895, the first traditional Chinese New Year parade was held in Old Chinatown, weaving its way down an unpaved Marchessault Street.

一八九五年，第一屆中國新年遊行在舊中國城舉行，遊行隊伍行在馬其索街的原始道路上。

Photo courtesy of Seaver Center for Western History Research, Natural History Museum of Los Angeles County

Chinese children with long hair queues in Chinatown, circa 1890. They are wearing typical working garb, helping their parents after school.

一八九零年時，華人兒童蓄長髮辮，放學後穿上工作服，幫忙父母。

Photo courtesy of California Historical Society Title Insurance and Trust Photo Collection. Department of Special Collections, University of Southern California.

Alameda Street at Ferguson Alley in Old Chinatown, circa 1898. Produce, live chickens and plants were commonly seen along the sidewalk. The taller buildings shown are on Los Angeles Street.

一八九八年，舊中國城Ferguson 巷的阿拉米達街。鮮蔬果、活雞和植物等，在人行道上經常可見。圖上較高的一座樓房在洛杉磯街上。

Photo courtesy of Seaver Center for Western History Research, Natural History Museum of Los Angeles County

Living quarters in Old Chinatown in 1889. Chinatown's economic condition was poor. Insufficient water and drainage facilities resulted in sanitation problems. Most of the living quarters were flimsy wooden shacks with poor lighting and ventilation. Old Chinatown was densely inhabited by more than half of the 2000 Chinese then residing in Los Angeles.

一八八九年舊中國城的房舍。中國城的經濟貧困，排水設施不足，造成衛生問題。有些住處用薄木搭建，採光通風簡陋。舊中國城居住擁擠，當時二千華人中有半數以上都住在此地，然後才遷居洛杉磯。

Photo courtesy of El Pueblo de Los Angeles Historical Monument, Chinese American Museum Collection.

寂寞的辮子

8

### ▶ Chinese Laundries

Many Chinese entered into the laundry business. And, most people came to associate Chinese people with "laundry." One of the reasons many Chinese chose laundry as their business was because it took little capital to operate - one only needed soap, a scrub board, an iron and an ironing board.[9] The price for laundering shirts dropped to ten cents each versus the fifteen cents charged by other Americans. Most Chinese laundrymen worked at least 12 hours a day and often roomed in the store where they worked.

In 1872, the Los Angeles City Council passed a $5 license tax ordinance on hand laundry businesses. Most of the 15 Chinese laundries refused to pay. Their proprietors were arrested and taken to court, where some paid the taxes, others served five-day jail terms instead of paying. Despite regulations, the number of Chinese-owned and operated laundries reached a peak of 52 in the city in 1890, with an estimated employment of more than 500 people.[10] By 1896, the Wong and Lew families were running a chain of 35 laundries that employed many local Chinatown residents.[11] Chinese became closely associated with the laundry business. It was one of their predominant occupations for well over half a century.

### 洗衣業

許多華人當時投身洗衣業，提及華人，即使人連想到洗衣業。許多華人選擇經營洗衣店的原因之一是洗衣店的開業資本低，一塊肥皂、一張洗衣板、一只熨斗和一塊燙衣板就夠了，[9] 其他的美國店洗一件襯衫要價一毛五，華人的店裡只收一毛錢。大多數華工每天至少工作十二小時，而且經常就住在他們工作的店裡。

一八七二年，洛杉磯市議會通過徵收五元營業執照稅條例，手洗業者均受到影響。十五家華人洗衣業者大多拒絕付稅，店主們因此被捕，送進法庭，其中有的付稅了事，其他不付稅者，則在獄中服刑五天。儘管有管制法規，一八九零年時，華人擁有和經營的洗衣店多達五十二家，據估計，在洗衣店中工作的華人有五百多人。[10] 一八九六年時，王氏和劉氏家族經營的連鎖洗衣店共有三十五家，受僱的員工也大多是華埠的居民，[11] 洗衣業成為華人專長的行業，而近半世紀以來，洗衣業也一直是華人獨攬的行業之一。

By 1880, about 300 Chinese lived along Negro Alley, an area 50 feet wide and one block long between the old Plaza and old Arcadia Street. The Chinese business center from the late 1860s until the 1890s, it was a town surrounded by slaughterhouses, railroad yards and the old Mexican Plaza.

一八八零年時，大約有三百名華人住在黑人巷，在the Old Plaza和舊亞凱迪亞街之間，五十呎寬，一街區的地方。這是一八六零年代後期到一八九零年間的華人商業中心，四周是屠宰場、鐵路場和老舊的Mexican Plaza。

Photo courtesy of Seaver Center for Western History Research, Natural History Museum of Los Angeles County

11

The Chinese Mission School of the Congregational Church in Los Angeles on February 25, 1896. In the settlement's early days, missionaries brought Christianity to the Chinese community. The Chinese Mission School also fulfilled a variety of educational needs, helping both adults and children acculturate into American society.

一八九六年二月二十五日，洛杉磯公理教會的華人學校。在華人安定後的初期，傳教士們成功的將基督教帶進了華人社區，滿足了華人在教育方面的需求，讓大人和孩子們都能融入美國社會。

Photo courtesy of the Shades of Los Angeles Archives/Los Angeles Public Library

Sing Kay Store, a general merchandise store was built on Marchessault Street in 1890.

一八九零年，馬其索街道上的雜貨店Sing Kay Store。

Photo courtesy of El Pueblo de Los Angeles Historical Monument, Chinese American Museum Collection.

寂寞的辮子

Workers at a Chinese field house, circa 1898. Chinese immigrants had a near monopoly on the fresh vegetable business in Los Angeles. They grew vegetables on leased plots of land using techniques they had learned in the agriculture-rich Canton delta.

一八九八年的華人農舍，華人幾乎攏斷洛杉磯的生果生意。華人在租來的土地上，用他們在農業富庶的廣東學來的技術，自行栽植蔬果。

Photo courtesy of California Historical Society Title Insurance and Trust Photo Collection. Department of Special Collections, University of Southern California.

Chinese boy with basket, circa 1900.

一九零零年，提籃的華人男孩。

Photo courtesy of California Historical Society Title Insurance and Trust Photo Collection. Department of Special Collections, University of Southern California.

An upper-class Chinese girl wearing a silk robe and embroidered slippers sits in front of an herbal store in Old Chinatown, circa 1900.

一九零零年，一個家境寬裕的中國女孩，穿著絲綢衣裳和繡花鞋，坐在中國城中藥鋪前。

Photo courtesy of California Historical Society Title Insurance and Trust Photo Collection. Department of Special Collections, University of Southern California.

The original school building on Castelar and College Streets opened in September 1882. Now in a newer structure, Castelar Elementary School is the second oldest operating school in the Los Angeles Unified School District.

一八八二年九月，在佳士德樂和大學街的原始校舍。這是洛杉磯聯合學區目前仍開放且歷史最久遠的第二所學校。

Photo courtesy of Chinese Historical Society of Southern California.

## 1871 Chinese Massacre

By 1870, the Chinese population in Los Angeles County had increased to 234 with 172 in the area close to the Plaza concentrated along the Negro Alley, which was 50 feet wide and one block long and located between the old Plaza and old Arcadia Street. It was an area surrounded by slaughterhouses, railroad yards and the Plaza.

As the Chinese began to compete with white workers, the anti-Chinese sentiment became widespread and grew in intensity. On October 24, 1871, the infamous Chinese Massacre took place. Two disputing Chinese accidentally killed Robert Thompson. That evening, a mob of about 500 whites killed 19 Chinese and looted Negro Alley. Every Chinese-occupied building on the block was ransacked and almost every resident was robbed. The man who actually shot Thompson escaped punishment, and only a few of the guilty members of the mob were imprisoned at San Quentin for a short period. The massacre caused substantial losses to the Chinese.[12]

Los Angeles, at that time, was still a little-known "backwater town," and when news of the massacre and subsequent lawlessness spread to the East Coast, it became front-page headlines, even bigger news than the 1871 Chicago fire.

## 一八七一年華人大屠殺

一八七零年代,洛杉磯縣的華裔人口已增加至二百三十四人,其中有一百七十二人集中靠近在被稱為是黑人走廊的墨西哥的Plaza地區,黑人走廊大約在舊Plaza和亞凱迪亞之間,寬五十呎,長一個街區。這個城鎮的四周是屠宰場、鐵路工作場,和舊墨西哥的Plaza。

在華工與白人競爭的同時,排華的氣燄也在逐漸高漲和擴散。一八七一年十月二十四日,鮮為人知的華人大屠殺發生了,兩名華人在吵鬧中誤殺了一名叫羅勃.湯普森的白人,同日晚間,大約有五百名白人暴民殺害了十九名華人,並且在黑人走廊大肆劫掠,幾乎整個街區的每一棟華人建築物都遭到暴民搜刮洗劫,而射殺湯普森的真兇卻消遙法外,滋事的不肖暴民也只有少數人被捕,短期監禁在聖昆丁監獄,這次屠殺事件使華人社區蒙受極大的損失。[12]

當時的洛杉磯還是不為人所知的窮鄉僻壤,當屠殺事件與目無法紀的醜聞傳嚷至東岸,立刻成為頭版頭條新聞,甚至較一八七一年的芝加哥大火還要醒目。

The Chinese Mission School, circa 1895. The man dressed in Western clothing is possibly Reverend Ng Poon Chew, who ministered to fellow Chinese in Los Angeles from 1894 to 1898 before relocating to San Francisco, where he published a daily newspaper, the Chung Sai Yat Po. The banner to the left of the men has the text for the Lord's Prayer, while the banner immediately behind the group is a poem. On the table are hymnals and Chinese language texts of the bible.

一八九五年的公理教會華人學校。穿著西服的可能是Ng Poon Chew牧師，他在一八九四年到一八九八年間，為洛杉磯華人講道，後遷至舊金山創辦Chung Sai Yat報。在他左側的橫幅寫著上帝的祝禱詞，人群後方的橫幅上是一首詩。桌上的是讚美詩集和中文聖經。

Photo courtesy of California Historical Society Title Insurance and Trust Photo Collection. Department of Special Collections, University of Southern California.

Mr. Chung Wong was a vegetable peddler who sold the bulk of his fresh produce door-to-door in the city from a horse-drawn wagon, circa 1900.

一九零零年代，蔬菜攤販Chung Wong 在城裡挨戶叫賣新鮮蔬果。

Photo courtesy of Chinese Historical Society of Southern California.

A Chinese vegetable peddler, circa 1900s.

一九零零年代的華裔菜販。

Photo courtesy of Chinese Historical Society of Southern California.

### ▶ Railroad Construction

In 1864, Chinese laborers were brought in to build the Central Pacific Railroad. A few years later, a total of over 3,000 Chinese laborers were recruited to build the Los Angeles connection of the Southern Pacific Railroad, including the perilous 7,000-foot San Fernando Tunnel. In 1876 the Southern Pacific Railroad connecting San Francisco and Los Angeles was completed.

Chinese labor was instrumental in completing the project. However, this invaluable contribution went largely unrecognized. At the completion ceremony on September 5, 1876, at Lang Station in Saugus, not even one acknowledgment was made about those Chinese laborers risking their lives to complete the tunnel on schedule. Although the Lang Station building no longer exists today, railroad tracks, crossing signals and equipment still mark the site.[13] In the ensuing years hundreds of urban and rural Chinese, including railroad workers and farmers, moved to Los Angeles and the surrounding areas, only to face increased anti-Chinese sentiment.

### 鐵路建築

一八六四年，華工被引進參加中西橫貫鐵路的修築工作，數年後，三千多名華工被招募來此，建造南太平洋鐵路，包括工程艱險的七千呎長的聖弗南度隧道，一八七六年，南太平洋鐵路連接舊金山和洛杉磯的路段竣工。

華工對完成這段工程確有貢獻，然而，他們無價的貢獻卻未獲肯定。一八七六年在Saugus的Lang車站舉行的峻工儀式上，當局對於華工勤奮不懈如期完成隧道一事隻字未提。 當時的火車站現在雖已不復存在，但平交道旁的號誌和裝備則留下了永遠的標記。[13] 儘管族裔對立的情勢愈演愈烈，往後數年間，又有數百名城鄉華人，包括鐵路工人和農民遷至洛杉磯和附近地區，反華情緒有如火上加油。

寂寞的辮子

The Chinese Cemetery Shrine at Evergreen Cemetery in Boyle Heights, circa 1900. The shrine is the oldest surviving structure from the early Chinese presence in Los Angeles. It was designated as Los Angeles Historic/Cultural Monument No. 486 in 1990. Early Chinese went to the burial site to pay homage to the dead, burning paper money and clothing so the deceased could use them in the afterlife. In the 1900s, the Chinese would exhume bodies after they had been buried for a number of years and send the bones back to China for burial. At one time, this traditional practice became headline news in a local newspaper. Residents complained to city health officials about the Chinese pulling bodies from the ground to ship them to the Flowery Kingdom.

一九零零年，Boyle Heights長青墓園的洛杉磯華人紀念碑，這是洛杉磯華人存在最古老的紀念碑，一九九零年時被命名爲第四八六號文化紀念碑。早期移民來此悼念逝者，焚燒冥紙和衣物，爲往生後衣食之用。一九零零年代，華人在逝者入土數年後，會開墳撿骨，再將遺骨送回中國埋葬，此一習俗一度還引起本地報紙的大肆報導。居民們向衛生官員投訴，指稱華人將死者遺骨掘出，運到the Flower Kingdom。

Photo courtesy of California Historical Society Title Insurance and Trust Photo Collection. Department of Special Collections, University of Southern California.

## Education and Religion

Though most Chinese immigrants survived on hard work and skill, education was certainly a passport to a better way of life. Christian missions fulfilled a variety of educational needs, serving both adults and children, and introducing all students to Anglo-Christian values. During its heyday, Chinatown boasted eight missions. In 1871, members of the Congregational Church initiated a Sunday evening language school in their white clapboard meeting house on New High Street at Temple, attempting to reach out to the Chinese community. In 1876, the First Chinese Presbyterian Church was established (presently known as the True Light Chinese Presbyterian Church) at San Pedro and First Streets under the leadership of Ira M. Condit. In 1894, the Chinese Children's School was founded at 766 Juan Street,[14] and by the 1900 census, 44 children were enrolled in its grammar grade level. Some boys and girls attended Chinese school until seven or eight o'clock at night after their regular school day.[15]

The missions' educational programs helped Chinese immigrants acculturate to American society. Today, the True Light Chinese Presbyterian Church and the First Chinese Methodist Church are the descendents of the missions.

### 教育與宗教

雖然多數華裔移民靠著勤奮工作和一技之長可在本地安身立命，但教育仍然是提高生活品質的必要條件。基督教教會滿足了華裔成人與孩子們教育方面的需求，也使華人認識白人基督教的價值觀。在鼎盛時期，華埠共有八所教會。一八七一年，公理會教堂在新高街和Temple交口的會議室，開辦了一所主日語言夜校，計劃深入接觸華人社區。一八七六年，在Ira M. Condit的領導下，第一華人長老會（現稱眞光華人長老會）在聖彼卓和第一街交口處創辦成立。一八九四年，中文文學校在766 Juan Street開辦，[14] 根據一九零零年的人口普查，中文學校的文法班有四十四名學生上課。大多數的孩子們在正規學校放學後，接著在中文學校上課，直到晚上七、八點。[15]

教會組織推動的教育工作幫助了華裔移民融入美國社會。今日的眞光華人長老會和第一華人浸信會承接了當年教會的神聖使命。

The Methodist Chinese Branch Church on Los
Angeles Street, circa 1900.

一九零零年，洛杉磯街上的華人美以美教會。

Photo courtesy of El Pueblo de Los Angeles
Historical Monument, Chinese American
Museum Collection.

Chinese men in Old Chinatown, circa 1900. The 1882 Chinese Exclusion Act resulted in many male Chinese laborers being condemned to a life of bachelorhood, deprived of a normal family life.

一九零零年，舊中國城中的華人男子。一八八二年排華法案使男性華工成爲終身光棍，使早期移民失去正常家庭生活。

Photo courtesy of El Pueblo de Los Angeles Historical Monument, Chinese American Museum Collection.

The north and south sides of Marchessault Street, looking toward Alameda Street. Note the tower of City Hall in the background. A horse and buggy is tied in the street. A wooden plank is embedded in the unpaved, dirt street to serve as a cross walk, circa 1900.

一九零零年，馬其索街的北邊和南邊，朝向阿拉米達街。市政府大樓就在後方。有一匹馬和馬車拴在街上。有一塊厚木板放在街上，充當人行道。

Photo courtesy of Seaver Center for Western History Research, Natural History Museum of Los Angeles County

A group of Chinese men reading signs hung on a wall in Negro Alley, circa 1900. Written all in Chinese characters, signs posted on "The Wall" served as a community bulletin board.

一九零零年，一群中國男子看著黑人巷牆上掛著的告示。用中文寫的告示牌被釘在洛杉磯街中段黑人巷中的牆上，有如社區佈告欄。

Photo courtesy of Seaver Center for Western History Research, Natural History Museum of Los Angeles County

## Vegetable Peddlers

In the 1870s, Chinese immigrants had a near monopoly on the fresh vegetable business in Los Angeles. They grew vegetables on leased plots of land, using techniques they had learned in the agriculture-rich Canton delta. Working on commission, they hauled their harvest in horse-drawn wagons, selling it door-to-door throughout the city and transporting the goods to a small downtown produce market located on Alameda Street. The economic gain to the community improved the quality of life for the whole Chinese population.[16]

However, in 1878 various municipalities throughout the state attempted to enact poll taxes, commercial license fees and other methods of limiting Chinese trade and social mobility. The City of Los Angeles passed a new ordinance requiring Chinese to acquire a permit before selling within city boundaries. The peddlers went on a protest strike, and the city was forced to back down.[17]

As a result of the produce strike, the Wai Leong Hong (Good People Protective Association) was founded in 1879 as a means for the Chinese to look after each other. Members of this association in later years served as the backbone in forming the Chinese Produce Merchant Association of Southern California.

By 1880, there were 1169 Chinese living in Los Angeles County, and about 300 of them lived in the Negro Alley area. Most of the vegetables consumed in Los Angeles were grown by the Chinese during this period. Of the 60 vegetable peddlers within the city, 50 were Chinese.[18]

By 1891, eleven years later, the number of Chinese peddler wagons registered in the city of Los Angeles had more than doubled, to 103. Chinese workers leased farms southwest of the city, along what are now known as Adams and Washington Boulevards. Chinese vegetable peddlers delivering door-to-door by horse-drawn wagons became a common sight in Los Angeles, and continued to be for the next 30 years.

In addition to the produce business, the Chinese operated laundries, ran restaurants and herb stores.

## 菜販

一八七零年代，華裔移民幾乎獨佔洛杉磯的新鮮果菜生意，他們利用在農業富庶的廣東三角洲學來的技術，在租來的土地上種植；他們賺取佣金、靠馬車耕耘、在城裡挨戶叫賣、把果菜運送到阿拉米達街上的小菜市場，他們努力發展社區經濟成功改善了所有華人的生活品質。[16]

然而，一八七八年，加州的各級城市試圖以徵收人頭稅、商業牌照費和其他方法，限制華人的商業和社會活動。洛杉磯市通過了一項新條例，要求華人在市內販售前，必須取得許可，菜販們群起罷工抗議，市府被迫讓步。[17]

該次菜農罷工後，衛良公所（保護良民協會）於一八七九年成立，鼓勵華人守望相助，會員們後來成為南加州華人果菜商協會的中堅份子。

至一八八零年，洛縣共有一千一百六十九名華人，其中大約三百人住在黑人走廊。當時，洛杉磯人食用的蔬果大都是華人所種植，城內的六十家菜販中，有五十家是華裔。[18]

十一年後，一八九一年，在洛市登記的華裔菜販倍增，共有一百零三家。華人租用城東南區的農場種植蔬果，也就是現在的亞當街和華盛頓大道處，洛市華裔菜販駕馬車送貨到家的常見景象，自此延續了三十年。

除了蔬果生意外，華人也經營洗衣店、餐館和中草藥鋪。

In the early days, Chinese women were only seen in public at events such as Chinese New Year's celebrations, weddings and funerals, circa 1900.

一九零零年代早期的華裔婦女只有在中國新年節慶、婚喪禮中，才會公開露面。

Photo courtesy of El Pueblo de Los Angeles Historical Monument, Chinese American Museum Collection.

Chinese children at the Chinese Presbyterian School in Los Angeles, circa 1900.

一九零零年，幼稚園的稚齡華裔學童。

Photo courtesy of El Pueblo de Los Angeles Historical Monument, Chinese American Museum Collection.

# Chapter 2

## Chinese Exclusion Act

In 1882, the first Chinese Exclusion Act was passed, suspending most immigration for ten years. It was the first time in U.S. history that restricted a certain class of immigrants from entering the country. The Act forced the Chinese who were not working and living on farms and ranches, to isolate themselves in Chinatown, where they became involved in occupations geared toward serving their own ethnic community. This helped them avoid competition with whites. At the same time, it was difficult for Chinese to live outside Chinatown unless they lived inside laundries or as live-in servants. In 1884, the Chinese Exclusion Act was clarified to ensure that the wives of Chinese laborers would also be denied entrance to the United States. As a result, a life of bachelorhood was formed for male Chinese laborers remaining in the country.[19] When the law was renewed in 1892, a proviso called the Geary Law was added, requiring Chinese residents to register or face deportation.

It was a dark time in the history of human relations between whites and Chinese. The Chinese were made scapegoats for perceived economic problems. A dramatic example of such anti-Chinese activity was the expulsion of Chinese residents from Pasadena in 1885. It was caused by a downtown fire which was wrongfully blamed on a Chinese. Many Chinese families were forced to leave downtown Pasadena within 24 hours. As a result, some moved to the area now known as Los Angeles Chinatown.

## 排華法案

一八八二年，美國第一宗排華法案通過，禁止華人移民十年，這是美國史上第一次禁止某一特定族裔入境。此項法案迫使不在農場居住和工作的華人，將自己隔絕在華埠，從事以華裔為對象的服務業，這使得華人得以避免與白人競爭。同時，若非住在洗衣店裡，或做寄宿僕役，華人很難在華埠之外居住。一八八四年，排華法案言明，華工的妻子也不得進入美國，致使在美的男性華工只有單身一輩子。[19]一八九二年，此一法案繼續生效執行，並且再增訂一條例，規定華裔居民必須登記，否則將被驅逐出境。

這是史上華人與白人關係的黑暗期，華人成為經濟問題的代罪羔羊。一八八五年帕莎迪納市驅逐華人事件是最嚴重的一次排華事件。當時，有一名華人被指為是市區一場火災的縱火者，許多華人家庭被迫在二十四小時內離開市中心，很多華人因此遷到洛市中國城。

## *Chinese Exclusion Act Years in Old Chinatown*
## 排華法案時的舊中國城

### 1886~1920
### Chinatown Arson

In 1886 and 1887, arsonists started fires in Chinatown, burning great portions of the old Negro Alley section and destroying several of the old adobes and flimsy wooden shacks which had been occupied by the Chinese for twenty years. The arsonists went unpunished. However, within a few months those flimsy shacks were replaced with brick buildings. Between 1887 and 1891, Chinatown was expanded along Apablasa and Marchessault Streets east of Alameda, and along Los Angeles Street. It became a fairly substantial complex of brick buildings, densely inhabited by more than half of the 2,000 Chinese residents in Los Angeles.[1]

### 一八八六年 ~ 一九二零年
### 華埠縱火事件

一八八六年到一八八七年，縱火者在唐人街四處肇事，燒毀了一大片舊黑人巷，以及好幾戶華人二十年來居住的老舊泥造和薄木屋，卻未受懲治。然而在數月之間，這些薄木屋很快地改建成磚造房。一八八七年至一八九一年，唐人街沿著阿拉米達東的亞帕柏萊莎和馬其索街，以及洛杉磯街日漸擴張，終於形成洛市二千多華裔聚集、滿是磚造房舍的中國城。[1]

## ► Garnier Building and Associations

A two-story brick structure known as the Garnier Building was built in 1890 for Chinese commercial use. It functioned as a social, economic, political, religious and educational center. The building housed businesses and schools, and served as church and organization headquarters. In 1891, Hep Tuck Hong Company signed the first lease in the Garnier Building. Sun Wing Wo and Company shortly followed, becoming one of Chinatown's largest and most enduring businesses, which sold rice, tea, Chinese herbs and other dry goods. Later Sun Wing Wo expanded to include a prosperous wholesale and import business.

Due to a lack of police protection and political representation, the Chinese community found it necessary to form their own organizations to meet their social, political and economic needs. Nearly all Chinese then living in Los Angeles joined some kind of protective association. As early as 1890, the Chinese Consolidated Benevolent Association (CCBA), located in the Garnier Building, was formed to help new arrivals become adjusted and to advocate their political and social advancement. About the same time, the Wong Family Association was established to carry on the values of mutual aid and benevolence, but functioned primarily as a social center for its members.

The CCBA had many roles. It mediated disputes between various organizations or individuals, served as a liaison with the Chinese government, fought against discrimination, and regulated diverse legal and business transactions.[2]

The association was also dedicated in providing social services by running a Chinese language school and building the first Chinese Cemetery on First Street and Eastern Ave., in East Los Angeles, for the Chinese community. Whenever there was flood and famine in China, it functioned as an agency to raise funds for relief. The association was also the chief organizer of local support for the Nationalist Movement in China.

Another type of fraternal and political organization, the Tong -- which means a hall, a parlor, or a place to meet and talk -- was also organized in the early days for benevolent protection. Los Angeles Chinatown was home to three major tongs: the Bing Kong Tong, the Hop Sing Tong and the Four Families Tong. Other tongs were dominant in other communities. As the Los Angeles tongs became larger and stronger, they engaged in legitimate and sometimes illegitimate businesses. Some were transformed from protective tongs into fighting tongs. With protection and revenge as their goals, conflict between tongs and other associations was inevitable. This led to a major "tong war" in Los Angeles on Marchessault Street in December 1920. Three Hop Sing gunmen hid in a store. One known as Lew Quan Oon opened fire on Bing Kong Tong members, killing two and badly wounding a third. The conflict was over the "possession" of a pretty Chinese woman known as Lillie Lem Lee. The fraternal tongs had a violent history because of fights over the control of various antisocial activities. In 1920, of the Chinese population of 2,200, 175 were Bing Kong men, 120 were Hop Sings and between 200 and 300 were members of the Four Families Tong. [3]

## 加尼爾大樓和公會

加尼爾大樓是一八九零年建築的二層磚造樓房，供華人商業活動之用，也是社交、經濟、政治、宗教、教育活動中心。大樓內有商家和學校，教會和社區組織的總部也設於此。一八九一年，Hep Tuck Hong公司簽下加尼爾大樓的第一張租約，新永和立刻跟進，販售米、茶、中草藥和其他乾貨的新永和是華埠一家老字號大型商號，後來擴大業務，經營批發和進口。

由於缺乏警察保護和政界代表，華裔社區深感必須成立自己的組織，以滿足社交生活，和政經方面的需要。一八九零年初，中華會館創辦成立，會址設在加尼爾大樓，以協助新移民適應新環境爲創會宗旨，同時促進華人在政經社會各界的發展。提倡宗親關愛互助的黃氏宗親會大約也在同時成立，成爲會員們社交生活的中心。

中華會館扮演多功能角色，協調個人和商家之間的爭議，聯絡政府與社區，對抗族裔歧視，規範各類商業交易。[2]

會館也積極推動社會服務，如開辦華文學校，開辦經營華人社區第一家東區華人墓園。當中國遭逢旱澇和饑荒時，會館也籌募救災基金，此外，會館也團結本地力量，領導支持國民黨的革命運動。

泛稱爲堂的兄弟會和政治組織（代表集會談話的地方，如廳、堂、或一處地方），也是早期爲守望相助而組成的。洛杉磯華埠是三大主要堂的發源地：秉公堂、合勝堂及龍岡親義公所，其他社區另有堂口。堂口組織日漸壯大，從事合法生意，也有些涉及非法活動。有些堂口從保護性質轉變爲打鬥組織，爲求自保和復仇，難免與其他組織之間發生衝突，一九二零年在洛市馬其索街爆發大規模的堂口械鬥，三名合勝堂成員持槍藏匿在一家商店內，其中劉關宏（譯音）向秉公堂一方開槍，結果造成二死一傷。雙方衝突的起因在爭奪一個名叫李莉莉（譯音）的美貌華裔女子。兄弟堂口爲控制反社會活動常生械鬥，總無法脫離暴力活動。一九二零年，在二千二百名華人中，有一百七十五人屬於秉公堂，一百二十人屬於合勝堂，另有二、三百人是龍岡親義公所會員。[3]

寂寞的辮子

At the turn of the 19th century, the Chee Kung Tong, known as Chinese Masonic Hall, was located on 355-1/2 Apablasa Street in Old Chinatown. Through its secret political affiliations, the group raised funds to support the California revolutionary activities of Dr. Sun Yat-Sen against the Manchus.

十九世紀時，被視爲是華人共濟會的Chee Kung 堂位於舊中國城355-1/2Apablasa街。他們與盟友聯繫，爲孫中山博士推翻滿清的革命運動募款。

Photo courtesy of El Pueblo de Los Angeles Historical Monument, Chinese American Museum Collection.

## ▶ Geary Act

In 1893, the Geary Act required Chinese laborers to register with the federal government and to provide proof of lawful residency within the country. Failing to do so meant facing deportation. Wong Dep Ken, a Los Angeles cigar maker, was the first Chinese to be deported from the United States under this act. Due to ongoing anti-Chinese sentiment, Chinese were expelled from Cahuenga Valley (now Hollywood), Norwalk, Burbank, Vernon and Pasadena by local citizens.

## Geary 法案

一八九三年，Geary法案規定華工須向聯邦政府註冊，並提供在美國合法居留證明，違者遞解出境。洛市一個雪茄製造商黃丹坎（譯音）是依本法被驅離美國的第一名華人。由於持續升高的排華情緒，華人被當地市民趕出卡橫加谷（今日的好萊塢），諾瓦克、勃班克、弗納和帕莎迪納的情形也是如此。

A Chinese laundry man carrying wash baskets with a pole, circa 1902-1905.

一九零二至一九零五年，一華裔洗衣工人肩挑衣籃。

Photo courtesy of Seaver Center for Western History Research, Natural History Museum of Los Angeles County

The Lugo House on Los Angeles Street, opposite the old Plaza. Built in the 1860s, this was one of the oldest adobe houses in Los Angeles. It later was occupied by the Pekin Curio Shop and Hop Sing Tong until it was torn down in 1951 for the building of the Santa Ana Freeway.

The Lugo House 在洛杉磯街上，就在the Old Plaza的對面。建造於一八六零年代，這是洛杉磯最早的土造房，後來爲Pekin Curio Shop和合勝堂所在，一九五一年時，因修築聖塔安納鐵路而拆除。

Photo courtesy of El Pueblo de Los Angeles Historical Monument, Chinese American Museum Collection.

寂寞的辮子

Chinese children, circa 1912.

一九一二年，華裔兒童們。

Photo courtesy of Chinese Historical Society of Southern California

# ▶ Old Chinatown

By 1900, the Chinese population had increased to 3,209 in Los Angeles County. Chinese people were increasingly required to be self-sufficient due to their exclusion from Anglo economic activities. The four predominant occupations among local Chinese were in agriculture (44%), laundries (19%), restaurants (11%) and cooking (9.5%).

As a result of the bachelorhood caused by the Chinese Exclusion Act, only 59 Chinese households were actually recorded in the Los Angeles Census in 1900. China-born females were outnumbered by native-born Chinese females. Of 120 Chinese women, 66 were born in California and 54 in China. The major occupations for Chinese women as a whole were sewing and domestic service.[4]

In 1909, the Chinese had formed two major communities -- one in Chinatown next to the Plaza; the other in the City Market area. "The Plaza" became the center of the Chinese community. Old Chinatown's narrow, unpaved, dimly lit streets and alleys had coalesced over time into a residential and commercial community bordered by Aliso Street on the south, the junction of Alameda and Los Angeles Streets on the north, Olvera and Sanchez Streets on the west and the Los Angeles River on the east. Within its confines were about 200 buildings, including a Chinese opera house, a Chinese school, several restaurants, three temples, eight mission churches, a newspaper, its own telephone exchange and a produce market. It became an urban center for laborers and farm workers.

Opium smoking also allowed the few wealthy Chinese men a rich pastime at a cost of about $1.50 a day.[5] As early as 1909, Apablasa Street alone counted 34 businesses that were at least partially dedicated to opium and gambling.[6]

By the 1920s, some changes took place in the Chinese community economy. The Chinese vegetable peddlers faced the challenge of competing with produce farming on a large scale in the Imperial and San Joaquin Valleys. Refrigerated railroad cars brought tons of fresh vegetables into the area from the Imperial Valley, threatening the Chinese vegetable grower's livelihood. However, the Chinese peddlers gradually expanded into retail and wholesale produce businesses, greatly impacting the Los Angeles produce market.

## 舊唐人街

十九世紀時，洛杉磯華裔已達三千二百零九人，由於被隔絕在白人的經濟活動之外，華人日漸需要自給自足。當地華人的四大主要行業首先是務農（百分之四十四），其次是洗衣業（百分之十九）、餐館（百分之十一）和廚子（百分之九點五）。

由於排華法案之故，華人在一九零零年洛杉磯人口普查時登記的只有五十九戶，中國出生的女性人數超過本地出生的華人女性，一百二十名華人女性中，六十六人出生於加州，五十四人在中國出生，主要職業是車衣和管家。[4]

一九零九年，華人形成二大社區，一在華埠內，緊接 the plaza，一在市集地區。The Plaza成為華人社區中心，年代久遠老市區的狹窄、崎嶇又陰暗的巷道連接成住家和商業區，南至阿里索街，北以阿拉米達街和洛杉磯街交口為界，西抵歐維拉和桑奇士街，東可達洛杉磯河，區內有二百座建築物，包括一家中國戲院、一所華文學校、數間餐館、三座寺廟、八所教會、一家報社、一間電話接駁站，和一處蔬果市場，成為勞工和農工集中的市中心。

吸食鴉片是少數闊綽華人的奢侈消遣，一天大約一元五角的費用。[5] 早在一九零九年，僅僅在亞帕柏萊莎街上就有三十四家與鴉片和賭博相關的商號。[6]

一九二零年代，華裔社區的經濟活動有了改變，菜販必須迎戰來自帝王和聖華青谷大農場所生產的蔬果。冷凍貨運火車從帝王谷載入成噸的新鮮蔬菜，華裔菜農的生計備受威脅，為突破窘境，華裔菜販開始經營零售雜貨和蔬果批發生意，洛杉磯的蔬果生意因此大受影響。

The interior of Sun Wing Wo Company, general merchandise store, circa 1902.

一九零二年，新永和商品公司的內部。

Photo courtesy of Billy Lew and the El Pueblo de Los Angeles Historical Monument, Chinese American Museum Collection.

寂寞的辮子

Young Suey, owner of The Young Produce
Company at 351 Central Avenue in Los Angeles,
circa 1905. In the early days, the Chinese
dominated both the supply and the distribution of
farm produce.

一九零五年，為於洛杉磯351 Central Avenue的
The Young Produce Company的業主Young Suey
。早期華人獨攬農產品的供應和批發生意。

**Photo courtesy of the Shades of Los Angeles
Archives/Los Angeles Public Library**

## Founding of the City Market

In 1909, the congestion of wagons around the Plaza forced the market to move to Third and Central Streets; then to Sixth and Alameda Streets. Many Chinese looked toward building a new 10-acre wholesale produce market at the intersection of Ninth and San Pedro Streets, the area which later became known as the City Market. [7]

To launch the project, Louie Gwan donated 1,000 shares at a dollar per share. The City Market of Los Angeles was formed on April 13, 1909 and was headed by President Edward John Fleming, former City Attorney of Los Angeles. Four days later it opened under the united efforts of three racial groups: whites, Chinese and Japanese. Of the 44 dealers, 20 were Chinese. The surnames of Jong, Louie and Woo were prominent among the hardworking produce dealers and farmers. Henry A.G. Jong was credited with organizing the farmers and starting the market's produce business. In 1917 he was elected vice president of the organization.

The Chinese influence on Los Angeles's produce industry peaked in the 1910s with the Chinese dominating both the supply and the distribution of farm produce. The total number of Chinese-owned produce houses, including those occupying yard stalls, was about 100. More than 400 Chinese people were engaged in farming in and around the city of Los Angeles. The produce industry also gave Chinese Americans the opportunity to develop as wholesalers and brokers. In December of 1910, the City Market declared its first stock dividend of three cents a share.

As more families of the produce owners and workers moved into the City Market area, the so-called "Market Chinatown" grew. The neighborhood community provided housing, restaurants, grocery stores, laundries, barbershops, medical services (including herbalists), recreation halls, family and district associations, churches and Chinese schools.

Along San Pedro Street, restaurants like Tai Loy, Man Fook Low and Modern Café, and grocery stores like Wing Chong Lung and Ying Chong Lung were established by Chinese Americans for Chinese Americans. After ninety years of operation, the continuing success of the city market is due to the close cooperation of the Fleming, Louie and Jong families and its shareholders. Currently about 20 percent of the produce store owners in the City Market are Chinese. The City Market of Los Angeles is currently headed by Peter Fleming, president and CEO, Howard Jong, vice president, and Lester Chew, secretary and treasurer.

## 市集形成

一九零九年，成群的馬車圍繞在the Plaza，市集先遷至三街和中央街，再移至六街和阿拉米達街。許多華人不喜歡六街與阿拉米達街的擁擠，考慮在九街和聖彼卓街交口興建一處占地十畝的蔬果批發市場，該區也就是日後所稱的市集。[7]

初期為推動計劃，呂關以每股一元捐出一千股，洛杉磯市集就在一九零九年四月十三日成立，由前洛市檢察長Edward John Fleming擔任總裁，四天後，在白人、華人和日人三大族裔協力下，市集開張，四十四家經銷商中有二十家為華人，張、雷、吳氏主導榮農和蔬果經銷，Henry A. G. Jong對組織果榮農和開展市集蔬果生意有功，一九一七年被推選為副總裁。

一九一零年代，華商主導農場蔬果供應批發，對洛杉磯蔬果業的影響到達頂峰。包括在自家庭院種植者在內，華人擁有的蔬果農場共有一百家，有四百多華人在洛市市內或近郊種植蔬果。蔬果業使華人有機會發展成為批發商和仲介商。一九一零年十二月，市集宣佈派發首次股東紅利，每股三分。

蔬果農場業主和農工陸續遷入市集一帶，華埠市集不斷擴大。臨近社區有住家房舍、餐館、雜貨行、洗衣店、理髮院、診所（包括中醫師）、遊樂設施、家族和社區協會、教會和華文學校。

沿聖彼卓街而下，中國餐館如Tai Loy、萬福樓、現代咖啡，和雜貨行如永昌隆和英昌隆，一路都是華商的生意。九十多年來，市集經營有成應歸功於Fleming，及雷、張氏與股東們的通力合作。今日，市集的蔬果業者仍有百分之二十是華裔。洛杉磯市集現任總裁為Peter Fleming、Howard Jong為副總裁，Lester Chew為秘書和財務。

Seven Chinese men and boys walking with
musical instruments in Ferguson Alley on Los
Angeles Street, circa 1910s.

一九一零年，七個華人男子和男童拿著樂器，
走在洛杉磯街Ferguson Alley。

Photo courtesy of Seaver Center for Western
History Research, Natural History Museum of
Los Angeles County

Louie Lee, a Chinese vegetable man, stands at 37
Westmoreland Place in 1909. etc. Such wagons
loaded with boxes of vegetables and baskets,
were once a common sight in Los Angeles.

一九零九年，華裔果菜商Louie Lee站在37
Westmoreland Place，他身旁的白馬和馬車
裝滿了成箱的果菜，這是當時洛杉磯常見
的景像。

Photo courtesy of Seaver Center for Western
History Research, Natural History Museum of
Los Angeles County

A dragon float filled with Chinese American children, circa 1903. This float may have been used in the parade to welcome President Theodore Roosevelt to Los Angeles in 1903.

一九零三年，一艘滿載華裔兒童的龍舟。這艘船可能於一九零三年在用於歡迎羅斯福總統的遊行。

Photo courtesy of Seaver Center for Western History Research, Natural History Museum of Los Angeles County

## ▶ Economic Conditions

By 1910, the original Chinatown had at least 15 Chinese restaurants mostly catering to non-Chinese customers, 17 Chinese produce companies, many Chinese gift shops, numerous grocery stores, wholesale art goods stores, medical offices and a variety of Chinese organizations. Chinatown not only served the Chinese community, but by the beginning of the century, it also began to be a tourist attraction.

Although Chinatown's economic condition was improving, water and drainage facilities were less abundant in the area. In 1914 the State Commission of Immigration and Housing reported that of the 252 Chinese apartments studied, 133 units had toilets in the kitchens since plumbing was being directed to only one part of the house. Other living conditions posed sanitation problems as well. Lack of code enforcement, inadequate municipal services and absentee ownership contributed to additional problems. Apablasa Street was situated in the flatlands close to the Los Angeles River. With only one drainage ditch and no flush tank in the larger area, health hazards ran rampant.[8]

## 經濟情況

到一九一零年，早期唐人街至少已有十五家中餐館，多數服務非華裔顧客，另有十七家華人蔬果公司、多家禮品店，和許多雜貨行、藝品批發商、醫生診所，以及華人組織。二十世紀初期，華埠不僅服務華人社區，也已經成爲是吸引遊客的觀光景點。

華埠的經濟情況日有改進，但排水設施卻明顯不足。一九一四年，國務院移民和住屋報告指出，在接受檢查的二百五十二棟華人公寓中，過半數（一百三十三棟）的房舍因整棟房子只有廚房與下水道通，馬桶竟安置在廚房內，其他方面的居住情形也因執法不力、市政服務不當、水電供應或缺乏業主管理，而有其他衛生問題。亞帕柏萊莎街近在洛杉磯河邊的平地上，卻僅有一條下水道，絕大部份地區又缺水箱，居民健康的惡劣環境難以想像。[8]

寂寞的辮子

# ▶ Construction of Union Station

The threat of Chinese relocation began in 1913 when the city proposed a new terminal for three separate railroads: the Southern Pacific, Union Pacific and the Atchison, Topeka, Santa Fe -- hence the name "Union Station." In 1934 work began on the $11-million Union Station, and many blocks of Old Chinatown east of Alameda were razed for the project. Thousands of residents already suffering the hardships of the Great Depression were forced to relocate to a crowded Chinese enclave near the City Market at Ninth and San Pedro Streets. Some-old timers held out, even after their water and power were cut off. Finally, Old Chinatown was mostly converted into railyards for the Union Station while a new China City and New Chinatown on Broadway were developed.

## 興建聯合車站

一九一三年，市政府提案，在經亞帕柏萊莎土地的南太平洋，聯合太平洋，以及阿奇森、托貝卡、聖塔菲三條鐵路線開新站(聯合車站命名由來)，華人被迫遷徙。一九三四年，耗資一千一百萬元的聯合車站開工，原中國城有一塊街區因受工程影響被夷爲平地，已受經濟蕭條所苦的數千居民不得不遷至靠近市集九街和聖彼卓街的擁擠華人區，有些老人家即使水電被斷也堅持不願搬離。最後，老華埠轉型成爲工業和倉庫區，而新城則沿著百老匯街逐步發展。

A brick building houses an herbalist and a barber shop on Marchessault Street between North Los Angeles and Alameda Streets, circa 1902 - 1905.

一九零二年到一九零五年，馬其索街，在北洛杉磯街和阿拉米達街上，一家中藥鋪和理髮店所在的磚造房。

Photo courtesy of Seaver Center for Western History Research, Natural History Museum of Los Angeles County

Vegetable peddlers selling produce at Jeanette Block on North Los Angeles Street, circa 1902-1905.

一九零二年到一九零五年，果菜攤販在北洛杉磯的Jeanette街區。

Photo courtesy of Seaver Center for Western History Research, Natural History Museum of Los Angeles County

## ▶ Social Structure

To show their loyalty to the new land, some Chinese men abandoned Chinese garb for Western costumes and cut off their queues, the form of hairstyle imposed by the Manchus as sign of loyalty to the Ching dynasty. Education was difficult to obtain for Chinese Americans. Women were trained to be the bearers of children. Due to anti-Chinese sentiments, Chinese women rarely went outside their homes and were only seen in public on special occasions such as the Chinese New Year, weddings and funerals. In the Chinese-American family in Los Angeles, wives tended to be much younger than their husbands due to previous immigration restrictions. The average age difference was 10.3 years in 1900 and 14.4 years in 1910.[9]

### 社會結構

為向新大陸效忠，華裔男子換下傳統服飾，穿上西服，剪去象徵臣服於滿州人的長辮。華人難有機會接受教育，傳統華裔婦女在家侍奉公婆、生兒育女。排華情緒使然，若非中國新年或婚喪等重要活動，華裔婦女鮮少在外拋頭露面。由於早年對移民的限制，洛杉磯華裔婦女多比先生年輕許多，一九零零年時，夫妻平均年齡相差十歲三個月，一九一零年時，相差近十四歲半。[9]

A delivery wagon parked out in front of a general merchandise store located at 802 Juan Street and operated by Mee Wo Chong , circa 1902-1905.

一九零二年到一九零五年，Mee Wo Chong的送貨車停在802 Juan 街，一家雜貨店前面。

Photo courtesy of Seaver Center for Western History Research, Natural History Museum of Los Angeles County

Looking down the south side of Marchessault
Street from Alameda Street, circa 1902-1905.
This area, once mostly occupied by Chinese herb
stores, is the present site of Union Station.

一九零二年到一九零五年，由阿拉米達
街看馬其索街的南邊。本區曾是中藥行
聚集之地，現爲聯合車站。

Photo courtesy of Seaver
Center for Western
History Research, Natural
History Museum of Los
Angeles County

Yick Hong Chung (left) with son Elbert (with bike) and workers in front of Mr. Chung's herb store at 917 S. Hill Street, circa 1909.

一九零九年，Yick Hong Chung（左）和其子Elbert（騎腳踏車），和工人們在他位於917 S. Hill的中藥鋪前。

Photo courtesy of the Shades of Los Angeles Archives/Los Angeles Public Library

寂寞的辮子

The Congregational Chinese Branch Church on 109-1/2 Commercial Street on September 12, 1908.

一九零八年九月十二日，位於109-1/2 Commercial Street上的公理教會華人分會。

Photo courtesy of the Shades of Los Angeles Archives/Los Angeles Public Library

Mrs. Ann Soo Hoo and family. (Left to right: LuLu, Peter, Mrs. Ann Soo Hoo, Mary, Pearl and Maye) They were wearing elaborate silk and satin clothing, headresses and hand-embroidered shoes for a special occasion in July 1908.

Ann Soo Hoo和她的家人們（左至右，Lulu、Peter、Ann Soo Hoo、Mary、 Pearl、和Maye）。一九零八年七月，在一個特別的場合，他們身著絲綢禮服和繡鞋。

Photo courtesy of the Shades of Los Angeles Archives/Los Angeles Public Library

An upper-class Chinese teacher and student, circa 1910s. At the turn of the century, men often coiled their queues around their heads. The queue was imposed upon the Chinese as a sign of subjugation when the Manchus took power in China in 1644. From the early 1910s to 1920, the queue became a fashion among Chinese men.

一九一零年代，上流社會的師生。本世紀初，男子多蓄髮辮，纏繞在頭上，蓄髮辮的習俗始於一六四四年，象徵滿清征服統治中國，一九一零年代早期到一九二零年，蓄髮成為男子的一種時尚打扮。

Photo courtesy of California Historical Society Title Insurance and Trust Photo Collection. Department of Special Collections, University of Southern California.

Upper-class mothers and daughters wearing the silk robes and embroidered slippers that signify a special occasion. Chinese women rarely went outside their homes. They were trained primarily to be dedicated helpers to their mothers-in-law and bearers of children.

上流社會的婦女穿著絲綢長袍和繡花鞋，參加特別盛會。華裔婦女很少出家門。她們自幼即被灌輸婦女應在家孝敬公婆和教養子女的觀念。

**Photo courtesy of the Shades of Los Angeles Archives/Los Angeles Public Library**

寂寞的辮子

Margaret J. Chung was the first Chinese-American woman physician in Southern California. She was born in Santa Barbara and graduated from USC in 1909. Dr. Chung was known as "Mom of the Flying Tigers" to hundreds of service men in the 1930s. After World War II, she devoted much of her time to serving as chief of China Relief's medical supplies division.

Margaret J. Chung是南加州第一位華裔女醫師。她出生於聖塔芭芭拉，一九零九年畢業自南加大。一九三零年代，Mrs. Chung被許多軍人尊稱爲「飛虎之母」，二次大戰後，她奉獻出大部分的時間，領導China Relief's醫療用品組。

Photo courtesy of the Shades of Los Angeles Archives/Los Angeles Public Library

In the early days, the Chinese would come to the altar, burn incense and paper clothing; leave food on the altar and toss paper money into the furnaces so that the family ancestors had plenty to wear and spend in the after life.

華裔祭拜祖先，會將食物放在祭壇上，將紙衣紙錢投入燃燒的香爐中，列祖列宗在往生的世界則可衣食無缺。

Photo courtesy of California Historical Society Title Insurance and Trust Photo Collection. Department of Special Collections, University of Southern California.

Jenny Lee ( middle row, 3rd from the
left) and teacher Leong Cheong
(center). A typical class at the First
Chinese language school in Chinatown,
June 1917. Some boys and girls
attended Chinese school until 7 or 8
p.m. after their regular school day.

一九一七年六月，Jenny Lee（中排左三）
和老師Leong Cheong（中）在中國城的
第一所中文學校的教室裡。當時，孩子
們在正規學校下課後，會到中文學校上
課，直到晚上七、八點。

Photo courtesy of the Shades of
Los Angeles Archives/Los Angeles
Public Library

Horse-drawn wagons were a common sight in the City Market on San Pedro Street, circa 1910s.

一九一零年代，聖彼卓市場的街上，馬車是常見的景像。

Photo courtesy of El Pueblo de Los Angeles Historical Monument, Chinese American Museum Collection.

### ▶ Chinese American Citizens Alliance

The Native Sons of the Golden State was founded in San Francisco in 1895 by a group of Chinese Americans who were denied admittance into the Native Sons of the Golden West, a fraternal order, because of their race. Membership consisted of naturalized and native-born Chinese Americans who fought for voting rights for U.S. citizens of Chinese ancestry, for the repeal of the Chinese Exclusion Act, for integration of Chinese children into public schools and for an end to discriminatory regulations against Chinese businesses. From its headquarters in San Francisco, a number of local lodges were established in various cities across the United States. The Los Angeles Lodge was founded in 1912. The name of the organization was changed to its present name, the Chinese American Citizens Alliance, in 1915. Today the Los Angeles Lodge is one of the largest and most active lodges monitoring and helping develop local legislation, citizenship education, and voter registration on behalf of Chinese Americans.[10]

### 同源會

一八九五年，一群華人因族裔背景之故，被拒絕加入一兄弟會組織Native Sons of the Golden West，遂於舊金山自組黃金加州子弟會，會員包括歸化入籍和本地出生的華裔美人，致力爭取華人公民的投票權、推翻排華法案、爭取華人子弟進入公立學校、終止對付華商的歧視法規。該會的總部設於舊金山，在全美各大城市都設有分會，一九一二年洛杉磯分會成立，一九一五年，更名為現稱之「同源會」。洛杉磯分會是目前全美組織最大、活動最積極的分會之一，支持華人參政、提倡公民教育、推動選民登記。[10]

Thomas Ung (1st on the right with a cigar in his hand), one of the produce owners, and the three Don brothers (center of the 1st row) at the Los Angeles Produce Company 1910.

一九一零年，Los Angeles Produce Company 的所有人之一Thomas Ung(右一手持雪茄)和Don 氏兄弟(前排中)在公司前。

Photo courtesy of Chinese Historical Society of Southern California

Chinese Presbyterian School and Lew Way's blacksmith shop, circa 1913.

一九一三年，華人長老會學校和 Lew Way's Blacksmith店。

Photo courtesy of El Pueblo de Los Angeles Historical Monument, Chinese American Museum Collection.

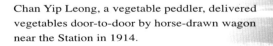

Chan Yip Leong, a vegetable peddler, delivered vegetables door-to-door by horse-drawn wagon near the Station in 1914.

一九一四年，蔬果攤販Chan Yip Leong在靠近聯合車站旁，駕著馬車挨戶送蔬果。

Photo courtesy of the Shades of Los Angeles Archives/Los Angeles Public Library

Mr. Lambert Fong and his son with a wagon in front of a cigar store known as Ten Chong Co., circa 1916.

一九一六年，Lambert Fong和兒子在 Ten Chong Co. 煙草鋪前。

Photo courtesy of El Pueblo de Los Angeles Historical Monument, Chinese American Museum Collection.

Sam Chung working on his father's (Yick Hong Chung's) asparagus farm in the San Fernando Valley, circa 1917. At that time, most Chinese farmers leased farms outside the city.

一九一七年，Sam Chung在其父（Yick Hong Chung）位於 聖弗南度谷的蘆筍農場上工作。當時有許多華人農夫在城外 租地耕作。

Photo courtesy of the Shades of Los Angeles Archives/Los Angeles Public Library

寂寞的辮子

# *Chapter 3*

*Social Conditions in Old Chinatown*
舊華埠社會

寂寞的辮子

## ▶ The 1920s

In 1922, Old Chinatown only had two paved streets and 13 unpaved thoroughfares. It contained 184 shops, most of them consisting of one room with living quarters in the rear. Many of them had poor lighting and ventilation with no heat. Some of these business establishments operated gambling houses, opium dens and brothels whose customers were not only Chinese but from the general population. But most were legitimate businesses such as grocery stores, restaurants, herbal stores, produce businesses, curio stores, bakeries, fish markets, churches and schools.

Much of Chinatown was residential, with families living in the back of their stores. At this time, Chinatown had the worst housing conditions in the city. According to the State Commission of Immigration in 1916, 878 out of the 1572 rooms visited in Chinatown were found to be totally dark and windowless. [1]

## 一九二零年代

一九二二年，老唐人街只有二條鋪整過的街道，其他十三條街都未經整鋪。城裡有一百八十四家店鋪，大多數只有一間房，後面另有一處可供住宿的小角落，這些地方採光差、通風不良、也沒有暖氣。部份商家經營賭場、鴉片館和妓院，招攬華人和其他族裔光顧，不過大多數還是經營合法生意，如雜貨店、餐館、中藥草行、蔬果行、古董店、糕餅店、漁市、教會和學校。

唐人街主要是住宅區，一家人就住在店裡或店鋪附近，這是華人居住條件最差的一段時期。根據一九一六年移民委員會的訪查統計，受訪的一千五百七十二間住戶中，完全沒有照明和窗戶的就有八百七十八戶之多。[1]

## ▶ Bachelor Society/Racial Prejudice

Significant demographic changes began in 1924. The court decided that Chinese women were not entitled to enter this country, even if they were married to an American citizen. Due to such laws, even Chinese women born in America could not be certain of their citizenship status. An American-born woman would lose her U.S. citizenship if she married a non-citizen. Because of the many years of exclusion, an uneven gender ratio resulted, and early Chinese immigrants continued to be deprived of normal family life.

In addition, Chinese were barred from owning land, from performing certain occupations, from attending American social events, and from joining school and business organizations. Taft Leung was one of the victims of racial prejudice. When Taft was a student at the University of Southern California, he tried out for the Trojan band. He was a good trumpet player and passed the try-outs. However, the band rejected him because he was Chinese. And being denied union membership because of his race, he was not offered a job at the Ocean Park Pier Dance Hall.[2]

## 單身社會/族裔偏見

一九二四年，人口結構明顯改變，法庭裁定華裔婦女不得進入美國，即使他們已與美國公民成婚。由於相關法令的規定，即使在美出生的婦女也不確定其美國國籍，而美國出生的婦女若與不具公民資格者結婚，立即將失去自身的公民身份。多年來的排華結果，使華裔社區的男女比例不均，早期華裔移民享有正常家庭生活的權利被無情剝奪。

此外，華人不得私擁土地、不得從事某些職業、不得出席美國社交場合、不得參加學校和商業組織。Taft Leung是族裔歧視的受害人之一。當時，Taft是南加大學生，想加入學校樂隊，他能吹奏小號，通過了初試，可是卻因是華人而被樂隊被拒收，另外，在海洋公園歌舞樂團工作必須是工會會員，由於族裔背景之故而不能加入工會，致使他喪失工作機會。[2]

Yuen Kee Laundry on the northwest corner of Sunset and Spring Street, circa 1920. In Los Angeles, laundry work was one of the Chinese population's predominant occupations for well over half a century in Los Angeles. Most laundry workers worked at least 12 hours a day and often roomed at the store in which they worked.

一九二零年，在日落大道和士丙令街西北角的Yuen Kee洗衣店。在洛杉磯地區，華裔獨攬洗衣店生意超過半世紀之久。

Photo courtesy of Seaver Center for Western History Research, Natural History Museum of Los Angeles County

The Garnier Block between Arcadia Street and the Plaza on Los Angeles Street was occupied mostly by Chinese businesses. Sun Wing Wo and Company was one of the largest and most enduring businesses, selling rice, tea, Chinese herbs and other dry goods.

在洛杉磯街上，從亞凱迪亞街到the Plaza，絕大部分都是華商，新永和和他的公司是該區最久最大的商家之一，販賣米、茶、中草藥和乾貨。

Photo courtesy of Seaver Center for Western History Research, Natural History Museum of Los Angeles County

The Fook Wo Lung Curio Company and Chew Fun Chinese Herb Store on North Los Angeles and Marchessault Streets, circa 1920s.

一九二零年代，北洛杉磯街和馬其索街上的 The Fook Wo Lung Curio Company和Chew Fun 中藥鋪。

Photo courtesy of Seaver Center for Western History Research, Natural History Museum of Los Angeles County

寂寞的辮子

## ▶ City Market

In 1924, the Chinese community raised an additional $100,000 in capital to expand the City Market area to 12th Street. The produce business was more than a local trade. Merchants sold fruits and vegetables to the out-of-town districts and even shipped to the eastern markets. Small trucks gradually replaced horses and wagons. In 1929, horses were no longer permitted to enter the City Market yard because of city health regulations. Produce workers were paid $20 - $25 a week.[3]

## 市集

一九二四年，華人集資十萬元將市集擴建至十二街。蔬果業已不再只是地方的小生意，業者將蔬果賣到城外地區，甚至運到東岸出售，小型卡車漸漸取代了馬匹和馬車。一九二九年，市區衛生條例禁止馬匹進入市集，果菜工每週大約可掙得二十到二十五元。[3]

The two chop suey signs indicated the restaurants of Man Jen Low, on the left and upstairs, and Tuey Far Low, on the right on Marchessault Street (east from Alameda Street), 1912. Tuey Far Low was in business before 1904, and Man Jen Low was established not long after. Both survived the demolition of Old Chinatown in the 1930s, and relocated to New Chinatown in 1938.

一九一二年，這兩個「雜碎」的招牌指向左邊樓上的萬珍樓和右邊馬其索街上的翠花樓（在阿拉米達街東邊）。翠花樓早在一九零四年前就開業了，萬珍樓也在不久之後開業，一九三零年代，這兩家餐館都逃過了拆毀舊城一劫，一九三八年遷至新中國城。

Photo courtesy of El Pueblo de Los Angeles Historical Monument, Chinese American Museum Collection.

## ▶ Women and Recreation

To supplement family incomes, in the late 1920s women began to help in family businesses and do odd jobs such as sorting produce or sewing in addition to taking care of any children at home. Visits to neighbors, relatives or friends were the only source of recreation for many Chinese women. Children also followed this pattern. Some boys and girls went home after school and worked in their parents' shops or restaurants until very late. There were and still are few recreational facilities in Chinatown.

However, Chinatown finally did get its own recreational facility in 1927. The Apablasa Street Playground was carved out of an old stable on the south side of Apablasa Street. It had swings, a slide and a small clubhouse to keep children actively occupied and off the streets. Margaret Cope, a Macy Street School teacher, was one of the prime initiators of its development.[4]

### 婦女職業轉變

爲了補貼家計，一九二零年代晚期，除了在家帶孩子，婦女也開始幫忙生意，做些整理蔬果或縫補零工。對許多華裔婦女來說，拜訪左鄰右舍與親戚朋友是他們僅有的消遣，孩子們亦是如此，男女童放學回家後，就在父母的店裡或餐館裡幫忙，一直到很晚才休息。華埠在當時和現在竟都沒有幾處娛樂設施。

然而，在一九二七年，華人終於有了一處娛樂中心。亞帕柏萊莎街南邊的一間舊馬房改建成了亞帕柏萊莎遊樂場，遊樂場裡有鞦韆、滑梯，和一間可以讓孩子們不需再在街道上遊玩的活動室。梅西街小學的老師瑪格麗特‧柯普是這項計劃的主要發起人之一。[4]

### Pioneering Chinese-American Women

In the late 1920s, professional Chinese-American women were hard to find. However, Louise Leung Larson graduated from the University of Southern California with majors in English and Journalism in 1926. With a great desire to become a writer, at age 21 she became the first Asian-American reporter for a major metropolitan newspaper, the Los Angeles Record, on July 15, 1926. Leung Larson was assigned to cover the Hall of Justice, the various courts, and county, state and federal offices. Her first big story was the Charlie Chaplin divorce case. She left the Record in 1929, and her newspaper career continued into the 1940s with stints at the San Francisco News, the Chicago Daily News, the Los Angeles Times Sunday Magazine and the Los Angeles Daily News. Some of her most prominent stories included events such as the tax-evasion trial of Al Capone, Albert Einstein's national crusade for disarmament and Madame Chiang Kai Shek's U.S. visit. [5]

Caroline Chan, a pioneering educator, was another rare example of a successful professional Chinese-American woman. During the 1920s, professional and lifestyle choices still were limited for the Chinese. However, Caroline Chan was fortunate to be educated at the University of Southern California. Her father encouraged her to select the teaching profession. Graduating with a Bachelor of Arts degree in English and receiving a secondary education credential, Chan was qualified to teach English at the high school level. Chan broke the racial barrier and was hired as an English teacher at the Ninth Street School educating the newly arrived immigrants. Chan excelled in her career until she retired in the 1950s. [6]

### 華裔婦女先鋒

一九二零年後期，華裔婦女幾乎無人從事專業，不過，Louise Leung Larson則在大學主修英語和新聞，一九二六年畢業於南加大，她一心想成為作家，一九二六年七月十五日，在她二十一歲時，她成為第一位在美國主要報紙─洛杉磯記錄報擔任記者的華裔女性。Leung Larson受指派報導司法院、各法庭、縣、州和聯邦各部會新聞，查理‧恰普林的離婚案是她報導的第一件要聞。一九二九年，她離開記錄報，一直在新聞界任職到一九四零年代，期間她接受舊金山日報、芝加哥日報、洛杉磯時報週日雜誌和洛杉磯日報指派的工作。經她報導的重大事件有艾爾‧卡朋的逃稅審判、亞伯特‧愛因斯坦的全國裁軍改革運動，以及蔣介石夫人蔣宋美齡女士訪美。[5]

教育界先驅Caroline Chan是少數成功華裔婦女的代表之一。一九二零年代，華人專業和生活方式的選擇依舊有限。Caroline Chan很幸運的能在南加大就讀，她接受父親建議，選擇教職，畢業時擁有英語學士學位和初高中教師證書，合格在高中教授英文。Caroline Chan打破族裔藩籬，在第九街學校覓得一職，指導新移民婦女學習英文，她在教育界的傑出表現一直持續到一九五零年代。[6]

The corner of Napier and Juan Streets where the Chinese farmers parked their horses and wagons after selling their vegetables at the markets, circa 1920s.

一九二零年時期，Napier和Juan的街角是華裔農人在市場收市之後停放馬匹和馬車的地方。

Photo courtesy of El Pueblo de Los Angeles Historical Monument, Chinese American Museum Collection.

Aik Tong, Chinese merchant in Old Chinatown.

舊中國城華商Aik Tong.

Photo courtesy of California Historical Society Title Insurance and Trust Photo Collection. Department of Special Collections, University of Southern California.

Herb stores in Chinatown treated both Chinese and non-Chinese patients.

華戶的中草藥店爲華裔和非華裔病患看診。

Photo courtesy of California Historical Society Title Insurance and Trust Photo Collection. Department of Special Collections, University of Southern California.

The Apablasa Street Playground, the first recreational facility in Chinatown, was built in 1927. It was carved out of an old stable and contained swings, a slide and a small clubhouse.

中國城亞帕伯萊莎街的遊樂場於一九二七年完工，是中國城第一個遊樂設施，外形像一個舊馬房，裡面有鞦韆、溜滑梯和活

Photo courtesy of California Historical Society Title Insurance and Trust Photo Collection. Department of Special Collections, University of Southern California.

### ▶ **Los Angeles Chinese Baseball Team**

In 1927, the Los Angeles Chinese Baseball Team was formed by 14 young Chinese Americans in Chinatown. In two years, the team began playing in semi-professional leagues. Some of the opposing teams at that time were the Pacific Clay, Palm Merchants and Redondo Beach Merchants. The Chinese team players were faced with a number of obstacles -- inadequate practice area, poor equipment, lack of support and understanding from the community, unequal competition with opposing teams, heavy work and school schedules. The team gradually faded out in the mid-1930s, but its strong spirit is still seen inscription on the George Tong Memorial Award plaque, which hangs to this day on the wall of the Alpine Playground gym in Los Angeles Chinatown: "The greatest failure is not trying your hardest."[7]

At the end of the 1920s, some Chinese began to move into better residential districts. One such area, near Adams and San Pedro Streets, became Los Angeles' third major Chinatown. At its height, the West Adams Chinese area extended from Central Avenue as far as Arlington Avenue.

### 洛杉磯華人棒球隊

一九二七年，十四名華裔青年在華埠組織洛杉磯華人棒球隊。兩年之間，球隊已和半職業球隊競賽，對手中有太平洋克雷隊、棕櫚商家隊和麗浪多海灘商家隊。球隊的競賽持續到一九三零年代中期，在此期間，球員們面對種種困難，例如沒有合適的球場、破舊的球具、缺乏社區的支持和諒解、不公平的比賽、沉重的工作量、上課時間衝突等，球隊逐漸解散。今日洛市華埠愛盼遊樂中心體育館的牆上還掛著George Tong的紀念獎牌，該是當年華人棒球隊堅強士氣的最佳寫照。[7]

一九二零年代末期，部份華人開始遷到較理想的住宅區，西亞當區於是成爲洛杉磯的第三處中國城，在鼎盛時期，西亞當華人區由中央街（Central Avenue），擴展至阿靈頓街（Arlington Avenue）。

Oriental Herb Company in Los Angeles,
circa 1920s.

一九二零年前後，洛杉磯的
Oriental Herb Company

Photo courtesy of Chinese Historical
Society of Southern California

San Pedro City Market, 1926.

一九二六年的聖彼卓市集

Photo courtesy of Howard Jong

寂寞的辮子

Mr. Jan Shiu Wong, a restaurant owner, and
his grandson Wing B. Wong in Old
Chinatown in 1921.

一九二一年，餐館業主Jan Shiu Wong和他的
孫子Wing B. Wong在舊中國城。

Photo courtesy of Nancy Yee

# *Chapter 4*

*The Birth of China City, " Chinese Movie Land " and New Chinatown*

中國市的誕生，〝中國電影製片場〞和新華埠

**The 1930s**

By 1930, 40 percent of Chinese Americans were native born. The first of a new generation began to make their mark on mainstream America. Young men and women were striving their best to be part of the mainstream society by seeking professional employment outside Chinatown and attending major universities. At the same time, the Chinese-American family was finding it increasingly acceptable and necessary for a daughter or mother to work outside the home. Chinese women and men started to organize themselves or join voluntary associations, such as the Mei Wah Club, Girl's Glee Club, Kuun Ying Girls Service Club, the Los Angeles Chinese Women's Club, C.A.C.A. Band, Men's Glee Club and the Guardsmen. These groups had the common goal to support social, sports, and philanthropic activities in the Chinese and other communities and to strive to bridge culture and sociological gaps.[1]

Confronted with ignorance and racial hostility, this generation of American-born Chinese searched for their identities and goals in both their Chinese and American worlds. Their achievements laid the foundation for future generations.

## 一九三零年代

一九三零年時，百分之四十的華人都是本地出生，華人新生代開始在主流社會發展，年輕男女胸懷理想抱負，或在華埠外謀職，或進入知名學府，漸漸融入社會。同時，華裔家庭也開始接受並感到有需要讓女兒或母親出外工作。華裔也逐步發展組織或協會，如美華會、Girl's Glee會、觀音會、洛杉磯華裔婦女會、同源會樂隊、Men's Glee會及the Guardsmen。這些組織的共同目標是提供華人和其他社區，社交、體育和敦睦活動，並消弭文化藩籬和社會隔閡。[1]

本地出生的華人子弟，身處被漠視與族裔對立的環境，努力在華人和美國世界中尋找立足之地，他們的成就為日後的華人奠下基礎。

The Louie Produce Company with Founder Tin Louie ( center ), Dan Louie, Sr. ( later owner ) and his son Dan Louie, Jr. ( 6th and 7th from right ), in the mid-1930s. Louie and his descendants were and are still prominent produce dealers and farmers.

一九三零年代的Louie Produce Company和創立人呂天（中），呂登（繼任的公司付責人）和其子呂國芳（右排起第六位、第七位），呂氏的後人成爲知名的果菜生產和供應商。

Photo courtesy of El Pueblo de Los Angeles Historical Monument, Chinese American Museum Collection.

A Chinese mother and a child hanging laundry in Old Chinatown, circa 1932

一九三二年，華裔母子在舊城晾衣服。

Photo courtesy of Pomona College, Claremont, Ca. Gift of Eliza Hart Leonard, in memory of Thomas H. Leonard, M.D

寂寞的辮子

Chinatown street scene, circa 1932.

一九三二年的華埠街景。

Photo courtesy of Pomona
College, Claremont, Ca. Gift of
Eliza Hart Leonard, in memory of
Thomas H. Leonard, M.D.

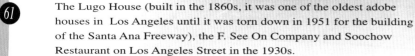

The Lugo House (built in the 1860s, it was one of the oldest adobe houses in Los Angeles until it was torn down in 1951 for the building of the Santa Ana Freeway), the F. See On Company and Soochow Restaurant on Los Angeles Street in the 1930s.

一九三零年代，洛杉磯街上的The Lugo House（一八六零年代興建，是洛杉磯最老的土造房，一九五一年時，爲了修築聖塔安納公路而拆除）、the F. See On Company和SooChow 餐館。

Photo courtesy of El Pueblo de Los Angeles Historical Monument, Chinese American Museum Collection.

The Lung Yeh's apartment, circa 1930s.

一九三零年代的Lung Yeh公寓。

Photo courtesy of Chinese Historical Society of Southern California

A Chinese Buddhist priest conducting a ceremony inside a temple, circa 1930.

一九三零年前後，一個華裔僧侶在廟裡主持法會。

Photo courtesy of California Historical Society Title Insurance and Trust Photo Collection. Department of Special Collections, University of Southern California.

寂寞的辮子

# ▶ China City

The removal of Old Chinatown to make way for Union Station in 1933 brought about significant changes in the community. Owners and developers discussed many beginning proposals and plans for a new Chinatown. Eventually two separate developments, a new Chinatown and China City, were constructed. Both were completed in 1938.

China City was located two blocks north of the Old Plaza, an area bounded by Spring Street on the west, Main Street on the east, Macy Street on the south and Ord Street on the north. China City was created for the tourist trade and was built with the support of Christine Sterling, a promoter of Olvera Street, and Harry Chandler of The Los Angeles Times. It was intended to depict a small Chinese village with an atmosphere of mystery. It featured quaint bazaars, shops, restaurants, lotus pools and gardens, temples and shrines on narrow winding streets and open courts. Visitors would rickshaw around the "city" and enjoy the rituals and traditional theatrical performances.

China City was called the Chinese Movie Land. It was pure Hollywood, complete with rickshaws and set decorations from the film "The Good Earth." In fact, hundreds of Chinese Americans were hired in Hollywood motion pictures. About one out of every 14 Chinese men and women in Los Angeles at the time had worked in movie studios.

Some patrons of oriental art curio stores - the leading business in China City at the time - came from the movie studios of Hollywood. These patrons became acquainted with Chinese in China City while visiting the stores, which were often open until late in the evening. They often called upon the Chinese they had met to be actors. Those who played an important role in a picture were paid at least $10 a day, and some signed contracts for several weeks.[2] Anna May Wong is a successful example of a Chinese actress in moving pictures. Her father operated a successful laundry in Los Angeles. Keye Luke, Victor Sen Yung and Benson Fong also were among the pioneering Chinese-American actors. The three of them had a combined total acting experience of 115 years. All portrayed sons of "Charlie Chan" in movies at various times. Bessie Loo was the first Chinese-American actor's agent for Asian talent in Hollywood. [3]

Johnny Yee, a member of the Chinese Historical Society of Southern California, recalled, "One could not forget the fragrant smell of temple incense, fortune tellers and the soft Chinese music as you entered the gate" to China City. At the Kwan Yin Temple, Yee would give a "free" stick of incense to each visitor who, after making a wish, would usually make a small donation to the temple as a gesture of goodwill. After visiting the temple, actress Mae West sent back an autographed photograph on which she wrote: "You must come up and see my temple sometime." [4]

In its first two years, China City was very successful and received the city's attention. However, it was destroyed by fire in early 1939. It was soon rebuilt, but in 1949 another disastrous fire demolished the main section of China City, permanently diminishing its glamour. It was never reopened.

Anna May Wong was the first Chinese-American woman to succeed in Hollywood, starring in silent films during the 1920s and 1930s.

黃霜柳是第一位走紅好萊塢的華裔女演員，在一九二零至一九三零年代的默片中主演。

Photo courtesy of Johnny Yee

## 中國市

一九三三年，為勻出空地以興建聯合車站，遷移舊中國城使社區有了重大改變。業主和開發商們商討了許多興建新中國城的計劃，最後決定興建一個全新的華埠和中國市，並在一九三八年完工。

中國市緊鄰艾爾‧普艾貝羅，該區北接士丙令街、東到緬街、南至梅西街、北達奧德街。中國市係為招攬觀光客和繁榮商業而設，獲奧維拉街地產商Christine Sterling和洛杉磯時報Harry Chandler的支持，期望在神祕的氣氛中，塑造一個小型的中國村。在狹窄的巷弄裡，中國村有古老的雜貨店、商店、食堂、荷花池和花園、廟堂，遊客們乘坐著黃包車川流其間，享受如電影中一般的景致。

中國市被稱為中國電影製片場，如同好萊塢一般，黃包車和現成的擺設讓電影美好的地球（The Good Earth）就地取材，好幾百名華人在好萊塢的電影中充當演員，當時，洛杉磯的華人中，每十四名男女中就有一人曾在電影或攝影棚裡工作。

東方骨董店是當時中國市最盛行的生意之一，顧客們多來自好萊塢的電影圈，店家多至深夜才打烊，經常惠顧使他們與中國市的華人日漸熟悉，之後，便邀請華人在電影中演出，在電影中飾演要角的每天至少可得十元，有些則簽下數週合約。[2] 黃霜柳即為華人女演員之一例，她在電影圈大放異彩，其父在洛杉磯經營洗衣業。另外，Leye Luke、Victor Sen Yung和Benson Fong也是早期知名華裔演員，他們三人的電影生涯共計一百一十五年，於不同時期，在電影中都被描繪成陳查理，Bessie Loo則是好萊塢第一位亞裔演員的女經紀人。[3]

南加州華人歷史學會會員Johnny Yee憶及當年，「沒有人能忘記當時走進中國市大門的香煙繚繞、算命先生和輕柔的中國音樂」。在觀音廟，Yee會遞給每一個訪客一支香，他們在許願之後，多會自由奉獻香油錢。進香之後，女演員Mae West送回一張簽名照，上面寫著「你一定要再回來看看我的廟」。[4]

在最初的兩年，中國市受到大眾的熱烈歡迎，經營有道，可惜好景不常，一九三九年初，遭祝融肆虐，夷為平地，但很快完成重建，可是一九四九年的另一場大火燒毀了中國市的重要地段，光華璀璨徹底灰飛煙滅，從此再未開放。

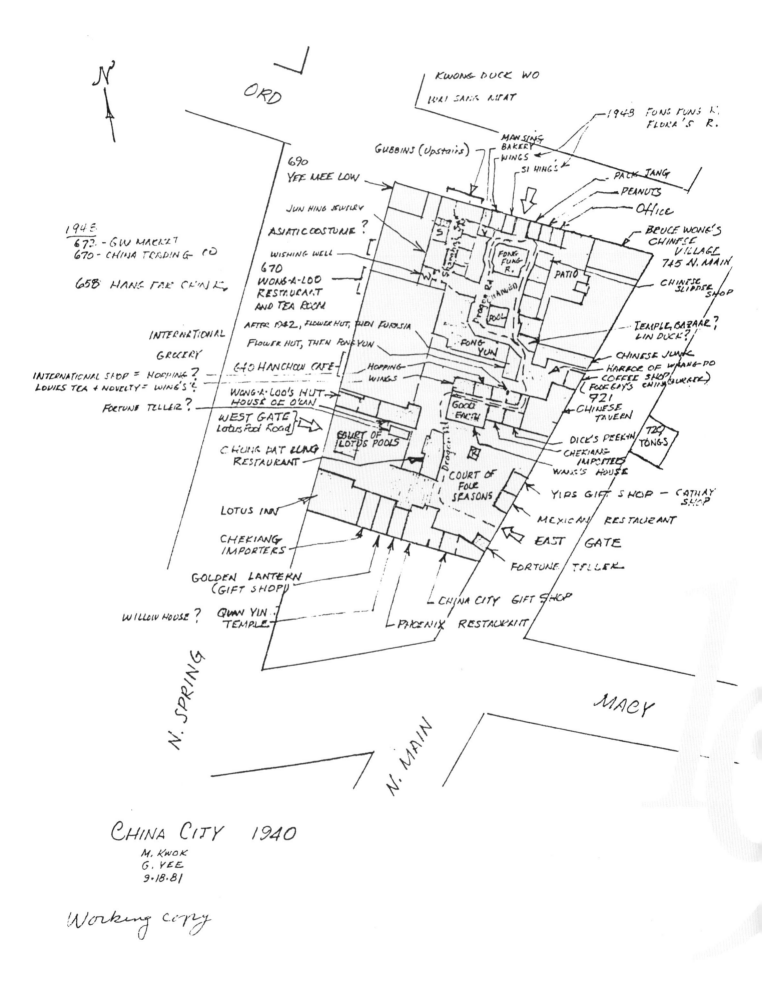

N

ORD

KWONG DUCK WO

KUI SANG MEAT

1948 FONG FUNG R.
FLORA'S R.

GUBBINS (Upstairs)

MAN SING
BAKERY

WINGS

SI HING'S

PACK TANG

690
YEE MEE LOW

PEANUTS

Office

1948:
672 - GW MARKET
670 - CHINA TRADING CO

658 HANG FAR CHONG

JUN HING JEWELRY

ASIATIC COSTUME ?

WISHING WELL

670
WONG-A-LOO
RESTAURANT
AND TEA ROOM

AFTER 1942, FLOWER HUT, THEN FUCHSIA

FLOWER HUT, THEN FONG YUN

INTERNATIONAL
GROCERY

INTERNATIONAL SHOP = HOPPING ?
LOUIE'S TEA + NOVELTY = WING'S ?

FORTUNE TELLER ?

640 HANCHOW CAFE

WONG-A-LOO'S HUT
HOUSE OF O'CAN

WEST GATE
Lotus Pool Road

CHUNG PAT KUNG
RESTAURANT

COURT OF
LOTUS POOLS

LOTUS INN

CHEKIANG
IMPORTERS

GOLDEN LANTERN
(GIFT SHOP)

WILLOW HOUSE ?

QUAN YIN
TEMPLE

FONG FUNG
R.

POOL

FONG
YUN

HOPPING
WINGS

GOOD
EARTH

COURT OF
FOUR
SEASONS

PATIO

BRUCE WONG'S
CHINESE
VILLAGE
745 N. MAIN

CHINESE
SLIPPER SHOP

TEMPLE BAZAAR ?
LIN DUCK ?

CHINESE JUNK

HARBOR OF WHANG-PO
COFFEE SHOP
(FOOK EAY'S CHINA BURGER)

721
CHINESE TAVERN

725
TONGS

DICK'S PEEKIN

CHEKIANG
IMPORTERS

WANG'S HOUSE

YIP'S GIFT SHOP — CATHAY
SHOP

MEXICAN RESTAURANT

EAST GATE

FORTUNE TELLER

CHINA CITY GIFT SHOP

PHOENIX RESTAURANT

N. SPRING

MACY

N. MAIN

CHINA CITY 1940
M. KWOK
G. YEE
9.18.81

Working copy

In the late 1930s, China City was created as a small Chinese village to attract tourists and the Hollywood motion picture industry. In 1949, a disastrous fire demolished the main section of China City. The last remaining structure of China City is the neon sign reading "Shanghai Street" on a wall on North Spring Street bordering what is now Philippe's parking lot.

一九三零年晚期，中國市被建造成一個小型中國村，以吸引觀光客和好萊塢的電影業。一九四九年，一場大火燒毀了大半的中國市，中國城僅存的建築物只剩下寫著「上海街」的霓紅燈招牌，現在成了Philippe's停車場。

Photo courtesy of California Historical Society Title Insurance and Trust Photo Collection. Department of Special Collections, University of Southern California.

寂寞的辮子

China City was called the Chinese Movie Land. About one out of every 14 Chinese men and women in Los Angeles at the time had worked in motion picture studios.

中國市被稱爲是中國電影製片廠，當時每十四個華人中就有一人在電影拍攝場工作。

Photo courtesy of California Historical Society Title Insurance and Trust Photo Collection. Department of Special Collections, University of Southern California.

The Chinese Congregational Church on 9th and San Pedro Streets in Los Angeles on April 16, 1933.

一九三三年四月十六日，在洛杉磯第九街和聖彼卓街上的華人公理教會。

Photo courtesy of the Shades of Los Angeles Archives/Los Angeles Public Library

寂寞的辮子

The Los Angeles "LOWA" basketball team on December 27, 1930. George Tong (backrow, 2nd right) was known as "City Hall" for his height in the Chinese community.

羅省華僑體育會的籃球攝於一九三零年十二月二十七日，George Tong（後排右二）因是華人社區最高的男子，被戲稱為〝City Hall〞

Photo courtesy of Margaret Ung and the Chinese Historical Society of Southern California.

North Alameda Street intersected by Marchessault Street, 1933. Chop Suey was a common sign for Chinese restaurants in Old Chinatown that catered to non-Chinese customers.

一九三三年，北阿拉米達街和馬其索街交叉口。在舊中國城，做非華裔生意的餐館常掛「Chop Suey」（雜碎）的招牌來招攬客人。

Photo courtesy of California Historical Society Title Insurance and Trust Photo Collection. Department of Special Collections, University of Southern California.

Looking south to City Hall along Olvera Street, November 1933. Big trees mark the Plaza, with the Sepulveda House and Pelanconi House on the right,

一九三三年十一月，沿著奧維拉街往南向市府望去。The Plaza四周爲大樹環繞，右邊還有Sepulveda House和Pelanconi House.

Photo courtesy of California Historical Society Title Insurance and Trust Photo Collection. Department of Special Collections, University of Southern California.

Edward Wong, a Chinese herbalist on 309 Marchessault Street, shown using the scales to weigh ingredients for a prescription. The unmarked drawers behind him hold the herbs. The Chinese used drugs such as quinine, digitalis and ephedrine long before Westerners discovered their value.

在309 馬其索街上一個華裔藥師Edward Wong用量秤配藥，他身後的抽屜裝有各種中藥。華人以奎寧、洋地黃和麻黃入藥，早在西方人之前。

Photo courtesy of California Historical Society Title Insurance and Trust Photo Collection. Department of Special Collections, University of Southern California.

# ▶ New Chinatown

Led and promoted by a distinguished civic leader, Peter Soo Hoo, and several local Chinese businessmen, a new Chinatown between North Broadway and Castelar Street (today's Hill Street), with Bernard and College Streets as its northern and southern boundaries, was built in 1938. Peter Soo Hoo acquired the property for 75 cents a square foot with the assistance of Herbert Lapham, a Santa Fe agent. [5]

New Chinatown was the first Chinese enclave in the United States which was owned by Chinese Americans. It was opened with 18 stores and a bean cake factory. The buildings were modern and built with earthquake and fire safety measures. It featured well-known streets with names such as Mei-Ling Way (the given name of Madame Chiang Kai Shek) and Sun Mun Way (for Dr. Sun Yat Sen's Three Principles of the People). Visitors entered the area through one of two large gates.

The East Gate, known as the "Pailou of Maternal Virtue", is one of the many famous landmarks in Chinatown on North Broadway. It was constructed from an authentic design by attorney You Chung Hong in 1938, and a plaque with four character poem of "The spirit of (Mother) Meng and (Mother) Ow" was placed by Hong to honor all mothers. Hong was heavily involved in the construction of New Chinatown, providing both legal advice and personal investments. [6]

Hong was also the first Chinese American lawyer to be admitted to the bar in Southern California. Both immigration law and his tireless work on behalf of Chinese-American civil rights were central to Hong's practice and life. For 50 years, Chinese-Americans regarded Y.C. Hong as the country's foremost Chinese attorney, a reputation based on his relentless work to repeal the Chinese Exclusion Act of 1882. He testified before the U.S. Senate Hearing Committee on immigration laws before he was 30 years old. At the age of 28, he was elected president of the Los Angeles Lodge of the Chinese American Citizens Alliance (C.A.C.A.). Hong also advocated his views on Chinese community affairs through the Chinese Times, the journal of C.A.C.A. [7]

The West Gate on North Hill Street features a column with a curved plaque with the inscription of "Dedicated to the Chinese Pioneers who Participated in the Constructive History of California", placed by the former Governor Frank F. Merriam. On top of the gate is a plaque with a four character motto inscribed "Cooperate to Achieve," composed by the Honorable T.K. Chang, the Chinese Consul at that time.

Chinese architecture and design can be seen inside the New Chinatown Plaza. The Golden Pagoda, now Hop Louie Restaurant, is one building from that time, with its elaborately overlaid Chinese detailing and upsweeping tile roofs and sculptures of mythical animals, such as golden dragons, are Chinese symbols of prosperity and protection. The project was owned and managed by the New Chinatown Corporation, which strived to create a community center that reflected an integration of both Chinese and American cultures. It catered primarily to tourists, and secondarily to Chinese residents.

The grand opening gala for New Chinatown was held on June 25, 1938. The area was decorated with colorful lanterns and banners, and the flags of the United States and the Republic of China were flown everywhere. To kick off the opening, a parade consisting of 400 Chinese youth in traditional Chinese costume marched through the area.

The Los Angeles New Chinatown Corporation staged the ceremony on Gin Ling Way at the West Gate on Hill Street. The master of ceremonies was Peter Soo Hoo. At the ceremony, former California Governor Frank F. Merriam noted that New Chinatown "represented a monument to those Chinese who played such an important role in building the West and a lasting evidence of American-Chinese amity." Illustrated articles in all the city's newspapers featured the public ceremonies, emphasizing the pioneering spirit of Chinese Americans. By its second anniversary, the mall was averaging 20,000 visitors a week. By 1942, the total investment grew to approximately $10 a share, a total of one million dollars. [8]

Chinese residents displaced to New Chinatown included a few pioneering entrepreneurs. The presence of the following businesses is testaments to their indomitable spirit. [9]

## 新中國城

位於北百老匯街與嘉士德樂街(今日的曉街的)的新中國城,在民權領導人Peter Soo Hoo和數名本地商人的領導和倡議下,於一九三八年興建完成,以佰納街和大學街為南北界。Peter Soo Hoo當時是以每平方呎七毛五的價錢,由聖塔菲地產經紀Herbert Lapham協助,購得這塊土地。[5]

新中國城是全美國第一個由華人擁有的華人社區,開放時就有十八家商店和一家豆腐廠。城裡的樓房設計新穎,通風良好,防震、防火、又衛生,街道寬廣,看來開闊又安全。大道多以人名命名,如美齡路(蔣介石夫人之名)和三民路(孫逸仙博士的三民主義),遊客須穿過這兩大城門才能進入城裡。

北百老匯街的東門又稱「母親的光輝」,是中國城內著名的古景之一,一九三八年時,依洪耀宗律師的特別設計建造。洪耀宗本人積極參與新中國城的開發建造,提供法律諮詢和個人投資。在東城門之上有一塊四字牌匾,由洪耀宗將牌匾安在城門之上,以紀念所有的母親。[6]

南加州及全美第一位華裔律師洪耀宗終其一生為移民法和爭取華裔民權不斷奔走。他畢生致力推翻一八八二年的排華法案,五十年來,華人推崇他為全國最傑出的華裔律師。年未及三十,他就在參院聽證會為移民法作證,二十八歲時,他獲選為同源會洛杉磯分會會長,以確保會員的和法權益和爭取平等政經機會為宗旨。他藉由同源會會刊中國時報,發表對華裔社區事務的看法。[7]

西門位於北曉街,由三個拱門、門柱和雕樑支撐的五塊天花板組成。前州長Frank F. Merriam特頒匾額「獻給參與創造加州歷史的華裔先鋒」,安置在西門的樑柱上。當時駐美大使T.K.Chang的「眾志成城」牌匾則置於城門之上。

時至今日,中國建築物的概念和特色在城裡隨處可見,特別是當年完工的建築物,如新中國城大樓內的金亭,現為Hop Louie餐廳,樓房使用西方建材,如磚、灰泥、水泥和木材,表現中國建築細緻的特色。未經粉刷的屋頂磚塊,有些尾端還有動物的形狀,有些裝飾華麗,或是建成數層涼亭。這些工程是由新中國城企業(New Chinatown Corporation)擁有管理,努力塑造一個反映中美文化的社區中心,主要是為了迎合觀光客,其次才是華裔居民。

新中國城的開幕式於一九三八年六月二十五日舉行,全市妝點著五彩燈籠和絲帶,美國與中華民國的旗幟隨風四處飄揚,身著傳統服飾的四百名華裔青年昂首闊步,行經觀禮台。

洛杉磯中國城企業(The Los Angeles Chinatown Corporation)將大會儀式安排在西城門旁金齡路和Hill街舉行,司儀是Peter Soo Hoo,在典禮中,前加州州長Frank F. Merriam致辭指出,新中國城是華人對開展美國西部的里程碑,也是華人對美貢獻的永恆見證。當時洛市各大報紙都以大幅圖文報導這項公開儀式,強調華人先賢的精神。新中國城屆滿二週年時,平均每週吸引二萬名顧客來訪,到一九四二年,總投資額已達一百萬元,大約每股十元。[8]

新中國城的居民不乏開路先鋒,以下商家們在在表現了華人不屈不撓的堅強意志。[9]

### ▶ K.G. Louie

K.G. Louie, one of the oldest gift shops in New Chinatown, was established by Mr. Ping Yuen Louie. Mr. Louie immigrated to the United States in 1917 and worked as a merchant in Stockton, California. In 1935, Louie moved to Los Angeles to seek a better life. He opened a store at 7th and Hope Streets and then at 4th and Main Streets.

In 1938, K.G. Louie was relocated to New Chinatown to help form the original nucleus of shops and restaurants. K.G. Louie is located on Gin Ling Way directly in front of the main East Gate entrance. Today, his family continues to operate the business.

### K.G. Louie

K.G. Louie由雷平原（譯音）經營，是中國城內發展初期的禮品店之一。雷氏在一九一七年移民來美，在加州的史塔克頓開店營生，一九三五年，搬到洛杉磯以尋求較好的經濟環境，他在七街和希望街開店，稍後在四街和緬街再開分店。

一九三八年，K.G. Louie遷入新中國城，準備開設禮品和餐館連鎖店，K.G. Louie就在東城門正對面的金齡路上。雷氏家人現接管經營生意。

The Chinese Moon Festival was held in Chinatown on October 8-9, 1938.

一九三八年十月八日和九日在中國城舉行的中秋慶祝會。

Photo courtesy of Chinese Historical Society of Southern California

This aged Chinese man takes his belongings from quarters that soon would be torn down. In 1933, Old Chinatown demolition was begun to make way for Union Station. Thousands of residents were forced to relocate out of Old Chinatown. Some moved to a Chinese enclave near the City Market at 9th and San Pedro Streets.

一九三三年，一位華裔老人家收拾行囊，離開即將被拆除的破舊房舍。舊中國城被拆除以便興建聯合車站。數千居民被迫遷出舊埠，有些搬到靠近第九街和聖彼卓街市集邊，擁擠的華人區。

Photo courtesy of Los Angeles Examiner and California Historical Society Title Insurance and Trust Photo Collection. Department of Special Collections, University of Southern California.

寂寞的辮子

Chinese reading news at the Shanghai Victory Bulletin. Screaming Chinese headlines posted on boards along narrow streets and alleys in Los Angeles Chinatown brought joy to old and young, rich and poor. They returned home happy to have access to this native language newspaper from San Francisco

華人閱覽上海公報上（Shanghai Victory Bulletin）的新聞。洛杉磯中國城大街小巷處處都張貼著醒目的告示，華人不分男女、老幼、貧富都非常興奮。他們帶著舊金山的華文報紙，高高興興的回家。

Photo courtesy of Los Angeles Examiner and California Historical Society Title Insurance and Trust Photo Collection. Department of Special Collections, University of Southern California

75

In the 1860s, long before this picture was taken, this popular restaurant was known as "Yue Yee Low" on Alameda Street in Old Chinatown. In 1938, Man Jen Low was forced to relocate its business from Old Chinatown to its present location in New Chinatown, where it became known as "General Lee's."

早在一八六零年代這張照片拍攝之前，這家餐館的原名爲Yue Yee樓，一九三八年，萬珍樓被遷到新中國城現址，改名爲李上校。

Photo courtesy of the Shades of Los Angeles Archives/Los Angeles Public Library

Yick Hong Chung (center) with his sons Elbert (left) and Sam (right) in front of Yick Hong Chung's Chinese Herb Company on 4925 S. Broadway in Los Angeles, 1938.

一九三八年，Yick Hong Chung（中）和其子Elbert（左）和Sam（右）在洛杉磯4925 S. Broadway的Yick Hong Chung中藥鋪前。

Photo courtesy of the Shades of Los Angeles Archives/Los Angeles Public Library

## Man Jen Low/General Lee's

Man Jen Low was first opened by Hoy Lee on First and Mateo Streets in Los Angeles and then moved to 3091/2 Marchessault Street in Old Chinatown in 1860. In 1908, Lee's son, Woo Fon Lee, was brought from China to help operate the business. A few years later, Lee returned to China and married Lum Shee. They eventually came to Los Angeles, and had eight children -- Kau, Rose, Walter, Norman, Merton, David, Jeni and one deceased son. Hoy Lee returned to China for retirement in 1927.

In 1938, Man Jen Low was relocated to its present location in New Chinatown. In 1941, David, Norman and Merton entered the military to serve in World War II. The rest of the family remained to help with the restaurant business while attending school. After World War II, the three brothers returned to continue operating the business. Mr. Woo Fon Lee passed away in 1950, leaving the business to the Lee brothers.

In 1954, Los Angeles Times food editor Paul Coates suggested that Man Jen Low should have an English name that would be "catchy" and easy to remember. Hence, the name "General Lee's Restaurant" was born. With new interior designing, delicious dishes and the best service, General Lee's became the most popular Chinese restaurant in Los Angeles. It began to receive many culinary awards and attracted celebrities and dignitaries from all over the world. The restaurant continued to flourish under the capable hands of the Lee brothers for almost 30 years. After 127 years, General Lee's finally closed its doors in 1987. [10]

The building at 475 Gin Ling Way became an unofficial historical landmark. It is still owned by David Lee. Lee is a past president of the Chinese Chamber of Commerce. He served as Airport Property Acquisition Commissioner under former Mayor Tom Bradley and is the current President of the Southern California Chapter of the National American Chinese Association. Lee is married to Yukie Lee. They have a daughter, Sharon, and two deceased sons, David and Steven.

## Man Jen Low/General Lee's

萬珍樓最早由Hoy Lee在洛市第一街和馬提歐街開張，於一八六零年時，遷到舊城馬奇索街3091 1/2號，一九零八年，其子Woo Fon Lee從中國大陸來此協助經營生意。數年後，他回中國和Lum Shee成婚，雙雙再返洛城，育有八名子女－Kau, Rose, Walter, Norman, Merton, David, Jeni，其中一子已故，一九二七年，李氏退休，返回中國。

一九三八年，萬珍樓被迫遷至新中國城現址，一九四一年，David, Norman 和Merton從軍，參加二次世界大戰，家人則一面上學，一面照顧餐館生意，二次大戰終了，兄弟三人返鄉繼續經營餐館生意。Woo Fon Lee於一九五零年過逝，生意傳給李氏兄弟。

一九五四年，洛杉磯時報的美食編輯Paul Coates提議萬珍樓應起一個炫目又好記的英文名字，「李上校」餐館於焉誕生，嶄新裝潢、佳餚美食，和親切的服務，李上校餐館成了洛市最受歡迎的中國餐館，美食評賞紛至沓來，吸引了世界各地達官貴人前往。由於李氏兄弟經營得法，往後的三十年，餐館生意也一直興旺，享有盛名。李上校餐館在中國城共一百二十七年，於一九八七年歇業。[10]

而在金齡路475號的樓房則成為民間的歷史路標，這幢樓房仍為David Lee所有，他是前羅省中華總商會會長，曾獲前洛市市長布萊德雷任命為機場土地徵收委員會委員，並為現任全國美華協會會長，與妻子Yukie Lee育有二男一女，女兒名為Sharon，二子David和Steven均已歿。

The 9th Street City Market celebrated its 25th
anniversary in 1935.

一九三五年，第九街市集慶祝二十五週年。

Photo courtesy of Chinese Historical Society of
Southern California

Jim (right) and Dick (left) Fong are the typical second generation children who grew up in the San Pedro/Adams area, circa 1934. Ponies were sometimes seen in front of houses for commercial photo taking.

一九三四年，Jim和Dick Fong是在聖彼卓市場長大的典型第二代華裔。兩人騎在收費拍照的迷你馬上留影。

Photo courtesy of Jim Fong

During the 1920s the Chinese Americans began to take an active interest in American culture. However, the leader of this all-Chinese band was Caucasian. Front row: 3rd from left -- George Chin, Back row: 2nd to 7th from left -- Taft Leong, Peter Soo Hoo, David Soo Hoo, Howard Leong and Lily Soo Hoo.

一九二零年代，華裔熱衷美國文化，但圖中全是華人的樂隊隊長卻是白人。前排左三是程達民，後排右二到七是Taft Leong, Peter Soo Hoo, David Soo Hoo, Howard Leong 和Lily Soo Hoo。

Photo courtesy of Chinese Historical Society of Southern California

夜婦女提燈隊攝影紀念 中華民國廿七年六月十日 美術照相館攝

The first Mei Wah Girls' Club in 1936. (Elsie is the first from the left.)

一九三六年，第一個美華女子俱樂部。（左一是Elsie）

Photo courtesy of the Shades of Los Angeles Archives/Los Angeles Public Library

A Chinese-American women's group gathering at the old Plaza in 1938.

一九三八年，中秋夜婦女提燈隊在the old Plaza前集會。

Photo courtesy of Delbert and Dolores Wong

### ► Chew Yuen Company

Chew Yuen Company was established by Kim Doon Soo Hoo at 308 Marchessault Street in Old Chinatown in 1916. The store sold various sundries including fresh vegetables displayed on the sidewalk. In 1938, Chew Yuen Company moved to 459 Gin Ling Way in New Chinatown's Central Plaza and gradually evolved from a general store to a gift shop.

### Chew Yuen Company

Kim Doon Soo Hoo於一九一六年創辦，Chew Yuen Company位於舊城馬奇索街308號，在人行道上販賣各式乾貨和蔬菜。一九三八年，Chew Yuen Company遷至新中國城中央大樓金齡路459號，由一家普通商店漸漸轉型爲禮品店。

The grand opening at the West Gate of New Chinatown, 1938.

一九三八年，新中國城西門的開幕式。

Photo courtesy of Chinese Historical Society of Southern California

寂寞的辮子

## Tuey Far Low/Grand Star Restaurant

The Tuey Far Low restaurant was established in the 1920s by Mr. Soon Doon Quon at the intersection of Alameda and Marchessault Streets in Old Chinatown. In 1938 the restaurant was relocated to the corner of Gin Ling Way and Sun Mun Way, where it was operated by his son, Him Gin Quon, for a few years. Tuey Far Low closed, but in 1946 Quon's grandsons, Wallace and Frank, opened another restaurant in New Chinatown known as the Quon Bros Grand Star Restaurant. At 93, Mama Yiu Hai Quon still cooked pan fried chow mein for crowds of hungry customers at the Grand Star Restaurant. In many ways, Mama Quon and the Quon brothers symbolize the Old Chinatown that has passed through its heyday and now is trying to carve a new niche for itself.

## Tuey Far Low/金星餐室

The Tuey Far Low餐館在一九二零年代由Soon Doon Quon開辦，地點就在舊城阿拉米達街和馬奇索街交口處。一九三八年，餐館遷到金齡路和孫文路交叉口，由期子Him Gin Quon繼續經營了數年。到了一九四六年，他的孫子Wallace和Frank結束餐館生意，另外在新中國城開了一家Quon Bros金星餐室。兩兄弟的母親關媽關媽媽一直到九十三歲還在為金星餐室的盈門食客做炒麵。關媽媽和關氏兄弟在很多方面代表著舊中國城走過艱困歲月，努力為自我打開新的局面。

The first anniversary celebration of New Chinatown in 1939.

一九三九年新中國城一週年慶。

Photo courtesy of The You Chung Hong and Mabel Chin Hong Archives

## ▶ The "Rice Bowl" Movement

The Women's New Life Movement Association was founded in 1938 in response to the Sino-Japanese war in China. The association collected clothes, money and medical supplies, and raised funds to relieve the suffering and starvation of war victims and orphaned children in China -- $2,000 to $3,000 each year. Along with the Women's Auxiliary to the Chinese American Citizens Alliance, many Chinese American women and girls assisted in organizing rallies and boycotts of goods made in Japan, and appealed to women to wear cotton hosiery instead of Japanese silk stockings. These launched a series of fundraising activities under the theme of a "Rice Bowl". The second generation Chinese Americans organized bazaars, fashion shows and theatrical and dance productions to raise money, while also providing the Chinese-American community with entertainment.[11]

Later in the summer of 1938, the Chinese Consolidated Benevolent Association conducted the first of the modern Chinese-American festivals in Old Chinatown, China City and New Chinatown. A three-day celebration of the Moon Festival with major parades held on the thoroughfares of Los Angeles connected all three Chinatowns to raise funds to support the China War Relief.

In 1939, the Chinese Patriotic Society boycotted Japanese goods and put an embargo on war materials to the aggressor countries. The whole Chinese community, including women and children, participated. The society went to the waterfront at Wilmington to picket ships that were chartered by Japanese agents to load thousands of tons of scrap iron to bring to Japan. The demonstration received nationwide attention.

## 一碗飯運動

婦女新運會於中國抗日期間在一九三八年成立。婦女新運會募集各界的衣物、善款、醫藥，並發動救災捐款，援助中國飽受戰亂和饑荒之苦的災民和孤兒，每年約二至三千元。許多婦女除了支援同源會，也協助組織社區會議，抵制日貨，並且鼓吹婦女穿著棉襪，拒著日產絲襪。一切活動在以「一碗飯」爲名的旗幟下展開。第二代華人則組織園遊會、服裝展示，和戲劇舞蹈活動進行籌款，同時也提供了華人娛樂活動。[11]

一九三八年夏季末，中華會館在舊中國城、中國市和新中國城舉行首屆現代中國節慶祝日，以爲期三日的中秋節慶活動，和行經連接三城與洛市大道的大規模遊行，爲中國救災籌款。

一九三九年，華人救國會發起抵制日貨和戰爭資源禁運至侵略國。包括婦女和兒童在內的全體華人社區都熱烈響應。救國會到威明頓的碼頭站崗示威，迫使日本船運經紀船隻拋下準備送往日本的數千噸廢鐵，此次示威在當時曾引起全美各界關注。

A group of Chinese traditional herb doctors at a meeting held by the Southern California Chinese Traditional Medicine Association in Old Chinatown on March 5, 1933.

一九三三年三月五日，中華醫藥會會議。

Photo courtesy of S.P. Lee Family Collection.

# Chapter 5

*Chinese Americans in World War II*
二次大戰中華裔美人

## Participation in World War II

On December 7, 1941, the attack on Pearl Harbor by Japanese planes and the resulting war signaled a turning point for Chinese Americans. For the first time, the 77,504 Chinese then living in the U.S., according to the 1940 U.S. Census, were able to enter the mainstream American society. They wore the same uniform and fought under the same flag for the same goal. One of five Chinese Americans served in the war. World War II gave Chinese Americans unprecedented opportunities to become part of the larger society during a time of need. It also gave them an opportunity to become naturalized citizens and obtain advance education through the G.I. Bill.

However, many Chinese people were afraid that they would be mistaken for Japanese, then the objects of American suspicion and hatred. In fact, some Chinese-American servicemen were mistaken for Japanese military and imprisoned until they could prove their identity. William Leung was one such World War II victim. He was almost shot by Americans while overseas, fighting the Japanese as an infantry machine gunner. Back home in Los Angeles, his sister Louise Leung Larson was taken to a police station when she was thought to be a Japanese spy. She was released when she proved her identity.[1]

During World War II, the United States and China became political allies. In 1944, the two countries worked together to build a ship called "China Victory." It was sponsored by Madame Wei Tao-Ming, wife of the Chinese ambassador in Washington, D.C. The Chinese deeply appreciated the cooperation of the America in helping to build and launch that ship. The act inspired a great number of Chinese in Los Angeles to rush to city harbors and join the shipbuilders in their important work. About 300 laundry owners in Los Angeles, comprising two-thirds of the total number of the city's laundry owners, closed their laundries to help fight the war. [2]

According to a report issued by the Selective Service in 1948, 13,499 Chinese Americans served in the armed forces of the United States from June 1, 1940 to June 30, 1945. On September 21, 1945, 16 of those Chinese veterans formed the Los Angeles Chinese Post 628. The Post was dedicated to providing readjustment assistance to returning World War II veterans, such as legal counsel on immigration matters and health care services. Other community activities included child welfare and higher education scholarship programs. [3]

## 參加二次世界大戰

一九四一年十二月七日,日本戰機突襲珍珠港,漸入尾聲的戰局似隱示在美華人的轉捩點。根據一九四零年美國人口普查,居住洛城的七萬七千五百零四名華人首次得以進入美國主流社會,穿著整齊的制服,在同一旗幟下英勇作戰,如所有的美國人,執行相同的任務,每五名華人中即有一人從軍。由於時局之需,二次世界大戰給予華人史無前例的契機,成為廣大社會的一份子,同時,根據退伍軍人法案,得以歸化成為美國人,並獲得接受教育的機會。

然而,許多華人擔心被誤為日人,而成了美國人懷疑和仇恨的代罪羔羊。事實上,除非他們提出身份證明,確實有些華裔軍人被誤認是日人而遭監禁,William Leung就是二次世界大戰的受害者,他是步兵機關槍手,在對日作戰時,幾乎被美國人射殺,回洛杉磯證實身份後才獲釋,又因被懷疑是日本間諜,其姊Louise Lung Larson甚至遭警方帶回問話。[1]

二次大戰期間,中美結為政治盟邦。一九四四年,在中國駐華府大使魏道明夫人的發起下,兩國合造了一艘船,命名為「中國勝利」,華人對美國人的通力合作、完成建造工程、下水啓航,深表感佩,洛杉磯許多華人湧向碼頭,加入造船的工作。其時,洛杉磯約有三百名洗衣店,將近全城三分之二的店主關上店門,一起協助作戰。[2]

一九四八年移民局的一份報告顯示,一九四零年六月一日到一九四五年六月三十日,共有一萬三千四百九十九人加入美國陸軍,一九四五年九月二十一日,十六名華人退伍軍人組成洛杉磯華人628軍隊,小隊為二次大戰解甲歸鄉的軍人們提供移民法律和醫療保健服務,並安排兒童福利和高等教育獎學金計劃等社區活動。[3]

At the Kuan Yin Temple of China City in 1941, 16-year-old Johnny Yee would give a "free" stick of incense to each visitor who, after making a wish, would usually give a donation to the temple as a gesture of good will.

一九四一年，時年十六歲的Johnny Yee在中國市的觀音廟前，遊客在許願、奉獻香油錢後，可以免費抽籤。

Photo courtesy of Johnny Yee

Johnny Yee holds a rickshaw in a production still in China City, circa 1941.

一九四一年，Johnny Yee 在中國城拍片時拉人力車

Photo courtesy of Johnny Yee.

Chinese theatre in China City
where Chinese traditional plays
were presented in English,
circa 1940.

一九四零年，中國市的中
國戲院上演著用英文表演
的中國傳統戲劇

Photo courtesy of Johnny Yee.

Gillbert and Donald Siu worked as extras in the Cecil B. DeMille's film of "The Good Earth" on July 4, 1940.

Cecil B. DeMille's的電影「The Good Earth」在中國市拍攝，一九四零年七月四日，Gilbert Siu和 Donald Siu在戲中扮演龍套腳色。

Photo courtesy of the Shades of Los Angeles Archives/Los Angeles Public Library

known to every inhabitant as "Tom Sook," which in Chinese means Uncle Tom. A Shanghai-born son of an Irish father, British mother, he operates a large shop of Chinese costumes and curios, but he spends most of his time counseling Chinese friends. They come to him about their domestic troubles, passport photos, hospital arrangements for expectant mothers. But probably his biggest service is

villains, Tom Sook has been on a spot trying to persuade his Chinese to step into the hated enemies' shoes. At first, all the money in the U. S. Mint didn't interest them. But at last they were persuaded when he pointed out that they'd really be helping China by portraying Jap villainy. But, like Luke Chang, shown with Tom Sook below, most Chinese make one stipulation: the Japs they play on the screen must come to a fitting, bloody end.

PHOTOGRAPH BY JAMES DOOLITTLE FOR THE AMERICAN MAGAZINE

One of the Hollywood casting agents, Tom Gubbins looked for Chinese extras to act as Japanese soldiers after the United States evacuated all Japanese. Luke Chan was one of the hundreds of Chinese-American actors in 1942.

Tom Gubbins是好萊塢選拔演員的經紀，在美國驅逐日人之後，他找尋華人來扮演日本士兵的角色。一九四二年，Luke Chan是數百名華裔演員之一

Photo courtesy of Johnny Yee

"Shanghai Gesture" was one Hollywood film based on China City that was produced in the 1940s. Chinese workers in China City were often called upon to act in moving picture roles. Those who played an important role in a picture were paid at least $10 a day. From left to right: Johnny Yee, Doris Chen, Edward Yip and Francis Chan in 1941.

「Shanghai Gesture」是一九四零年代好萊塢以中國市為背景拍攝的電影。在中國市工作的華人常被招攬去拍電影，扮演重要角色者每日可得十元美金，圖左至右：Johnny Yee, Doris Chen, Edward Yip和Francis Chan於一九四一年。

Photo courtesy of Johnny Yee

During the war years, many Chinese women had outstanding records in the sale of war bonds to support war relief activities, 1944.

在戰爭期間，於一九四四年，許多華裔婦女促銷戰爭公債，以援助作戰，成果輝煌。

Photo courtesy of the Shades of Los Angeles Archives/Los Angeles Public Library

▶ **End of the Chinese Exclusion Act**

As a result of the cooperation of China, Congress repealed the Chinese Exclusion Act in 1943, giving Chinese people eligibility to be admitted to the United States. A Chinese racial quota of 105 was proclaimed on February 8, 1944. Nevertheless, the War Brides Act of 1945 and the 1946 Fiancees Act significantly contributed to an increase in Chinese women immigrants, and soon a non-quota basis system permitted the entry of alien spouses and children born to members of the U.S. armed forces. This influx of immigrants had a tremendous impact on the demographics of the Chinese-American community.[4]

As the number of Chinese women in America gradually increased, both formal and informal sororities formed to meet the need for camaraderie. The Chinese Women's Club (CWC) was formed in 1947. Later, Mabel Chin Hong founded the Kuun Ying Girls service Club to enrich the lives of young Chinese women helping them understand the social and cultural ways of American life. Hong also headed the CWC from 1952 to 1954. In addition, women organized auxiliary activities within the Chinese fraternal organizations that had traditionally been for men only.

**排華法案終結**

一九四三年，由於與中國並肩作戰，美國國會決議廢止排華法案，予華人平等進入美國的機會。一九四四年二月八日，國會宣佈授予華人一百零五人移民配額，一九四五年的戰爭新娘法案和一九四六年的未婚妻法案，使得華裔婦女移民明顯增加。緊接著頒佈的無配額制度允許美國軍人居住在海外的配偶和未成年子女進入美國。新移民潮使華裔社區的人口結構產生重大的變化。[4]

隨華裔婦女人數增加，婦女之間正式和日常的交誼聯繫日形重要。為了滿足婦女在社交聯誼方面的需求，Mabel Chin Hong在一九四七年成立觀音女子俱樂部，一九五二年至一九五四年由她領導。此外，婦女也在華人互助會中舉辦傳統上只限男士參加的活動。

Madame Chiang Kai Shek
visited Los Angeles Chinatown
in 1943. The banner on the
Garnier Building reads
"Welcome Madame. Chiang."
The "Rice Bowl" campaign
reached its climax that year,
raising funds to support war
victims in China.

一九四三年，蔣宋美齡夫人訪問
洛杉磯華埠。掛在加尼爾大樓上
的橫幅上寫著歡迎蔣夫人。籌款
援助中國戰爭災民的一碗飯運動
達到最高潮。

Photo courtesy of El Pueblo de
Los Angeles Historical
Monument, Chinese American
Museum Collection.

寂寞的辮子

Mayor Fletcher Bowron and
Madame Chiang Kai Shek in
Los Angeles City Hall in 1943.
Madame Chiang visited Los
Angeles to raise funds for the
China Relief activities during
World War II.

一九四三年，洛杉磯市長
Fletcher Bowron和蔣宋美齡女士
在市府，蔣宋美齡訪洛為二次大
戰的救援中國活動募款。

Photo courtesy of the Shades of
Los Angeles Archives/Los
Angeles Public Library

### ▶ Madame Chiang Kai Shek's Visit

On March 31, 1943, Madame Chiang made her historic visit to Los Angeles to raise support for China. Her speech at the welcoming reception at the Hollywood Bowl inspired many Chinese American women to join the New Life Movement. As a result, the New Life's membership grew to over 200, and the "Rice Bowl" campaign begun in 1938 reached its climax that year. Chapters across the country raised funds, prepared medical supplies and collected clothing for the army and war victims in China.[5]

The war also created many jobs for women and racial minorities while the men were on the battlefield. Chinese Americans were given opportunities to work in aircraft plants, shipyards, machine shops, and even in professional and technical positions. However, it was not until the end of World War II that employers gradually began to hire Chinese to work in geographic areas not typically open to Chinese workers, such as West Los Angeles, Hollywood and Los Feliz.[6]

In 1948, the Supreme Court ruling barring restrictive covenants eliminated racial residential segregation. In May, some Chinese families moved into West Los Angeles, Hollywood and Beverly Hills, which previously had been occupied exclusively by Caucasians.[7]

### 蔣介石夫人來訪

一九四三年三月三十一日，蔣介石夫人抵達洛城訪問，募款支持中國。她在好萊塢碗的歡迎會的演說激勵許多華人婦女加入新生活運動，二百多人受感召加入爲會員，一九三八年的一碗飯運動將婦女情緒帶到最高點，全國各分會爲援助中國的軍隊和災民，積極籌款、準備醫療補給品和募集衣物。[5]

戰爭使男子遠征在外，也爲婦女和少數族裔創造許多工作機會，華裔有機會在飛機製造場、船塢、機械廠工作，甚至擔任專業或技術職位。直到二次大戰結束，美國僱主才漸漸雇用華人在非華人地區工作，如西洛杉磯、好萊塢和拉斯菲里斯。[6]

一九四八年，最高法院裁示嚴格禁止居住區族裔隔離，同年五月，即有華人搬到原爲白人居住的西洛杉磯、好萊塢和比佛利山等社區。[7]

Y.C. Hong welcomes Madame Chiang Kai Shek in Los Angeles in 1943.

一九四三年，洪耀宗在洛杉磯歡迎蔣宋美齡女士。

Photo courtesy of The You Chung Hong and Mabel Chin Hong Archives

The Moon Festival and Parade in 1941.

一九四一年，中秋節慶會和遊行活動。

Photo courtesy of El Pueblo de Los Angeles Historical Monument, Chinese American Museum Collection.

寂寞的辮子

Lim's Cafe (center), Tuey Far Low (2nd from right), Gin Ling Gift (right) and Wah On Company in New Chinatown, 1940.

一九四零年，新中國城的 Lim's Cafe（中）、翠花樓（右二）、金齡禮品（右）和Wah On Company。

Photo courtesy of Chinese Historical Society of Southern California

The Bamboo Inn Restaurant with owner Low Chew in China City in the early 1940s.

一九四零年代早期，中國市Bamboo Inn餐廳和業主劉照。

Photo courtesy of El Pueblo de Los Angeles Historical Monument, Chinese American Museum Collection.

The Mei Wah Girls' Club marching in a parade in New Chinatown, circa early 1940s.

一九四零年代早期，美華女子俱樂部參加在新中國城的遊行活動。

Photo courtesy of Chinese Historical Society of Southern California

Madame Chiang Kai Shek delivering a
speech in Hollywood Bowl in 1943.

一九四三年，蔣宋美齡女士在好萊塢演講。

Photo courtesy of Chinese Historical
Society of Southern California

寂寞的辮子

David Lee and his brothers, Norman and Merton, and other family members at Man Jen Low restaurant in the early 1940s.

一九四零年代，萬珍樓餐廳的 David Lee 和他的兄弟 Norman, Merton 及家人們。

Photo courtesy of David and Yuki Lee History Collection.

The American Legion American-Chinese Post 628 in 1946.

美國退伍軍人協會628小隊攝於1946年

Photo courtesy of S. P. Lee Photo Collection

Soon Doon Quon, a pioneer restaurant owner of Tuey Far Low, celebrated his 96th birthday with his son Him Gin Quon and other family members in 1945.

翠花樓的業主Soon Doon Quon於一九四五年時和其子Him Gin Quon及家人們歡度九十六大壽。

Photo courtesy of Wally Quon

## ▶ War Bond Sales

During the war years, many Chinese women achieved outstanding records in the sale of war bonds. The American Women's Voluntary Service (AWVS) Chinese Center/New Chinatown Canteen was formed by a group of Chinese American women with the support of the New York-based AWVS. The main goals of the center were to promote war bond sales, assist with various war and relief aid activities; and raise money to open a hospitality center in Chinatown for Chinese troops visiting the city. On November 28, 1942, the AWVS office was opened at 610 North Spring Street. The chair pro-tem of the center was Dorothy Siu, and Der Ling served as senior chair.[8]

Under Mabel Chin Hong's leadership, the Kuan Ying Girls Club devoted much of its time to entertaining the Chinese-American servicemen who came to town. These women worked in the Chinatown Canteen and raised funds for China relief. Hong oversaw the Chinatown Canteen as Corresponding Sponsor of the AWVS. On September 9, 1944, the New Chinatown Canteen was opened in the Leong family's Soo Chow Restaurant at 454 Jung Jing Road. For the next two years over 105 volunteer Chinese-American women worked to make it the "best home away from home" for American servicemen.

## 戰爭債券

大戰期間，許多華裔婦女積極促銷戰爭債券，頗有斬獲。一群華裔婦女在美國婦女志工服務會紐約分會的支持下，成立華人中心/新中國福利社，主要工作即促銷戰爭債券、協助戰爭救災活動，以及發動籌款，以期在中國城開辦一接待華裔軍人的招待所。一九四二年十一月二十八日，美國婦女志工會的辦事處在北士丙令街610號開張，Der Ling為會長，Dorothy Siu為副會長。[8]

在Mabel Chin Hong的領導下，觀音女了俱樂部投注了大半時間接待到城裡的華裔軍人。婦女們在中國城福利社工作，籌款協助中國救災。Hong為美國婦女志工會聯絡發起人，負責管理福利社。一九四四年九月九日，新中國城福利社在位於 454 Jung Jing 路的Leong家蘇州餐館開張，兩年內，即有超過一百零五名華裔婦女志願工作，給軍人們出門在外的一個最溫暖的家。

"Salute to Summer" is given by these members of the Colony of Orientals at China City. Left to right: Ruby Ling, Gilbert Sui, Charles Luck Jr., Sylvia Wong and John Wesley Luck.

東方孩子們在中國市行舉手禮。左至右，Ruby Ling, Gilbert Sui, Charles Luck Jr., Sylvia Wong和John Wesley Luck.

Photo courtesy of Los Angeles Examiner and California Historical Society Title Insurance and Trust Photo Collection. Department of Special Collections, University of Southern California.

The American Women's Voluntary Services was formed in 1942 by a group of Chinese-American women to promote war bond sales and assist the war relief program. Left to right: Anna Tom, Dorothy Lee, Alice Chow and Emma Tom.

一九四二年，一群華裔婦女為促銷戰爭債券以援助救災，成立了美國婦女志願服務隊，左至右Anna Tom, Dorothy Lee, Alice Chow和Emma Tom。

Photo courtesy of El Pueblo de Los Angeles Historical Monument, Chinese American Museum Collection

寂寞的辮子

Dr. Margaret Chung was pictured in her "trophy room," filled with souvenirs sent by American fliers in 1942. Dr. Chung was the first Chinese-American physician in Southern California in 1909. She was known as "Mom" to 465 of Uncle Sam's most brilliant fliers.

一九四二年，Dr. Margaret Chung在她滿是獎盃和美國空軍致贈的紀念品的房裡留影。一九零九年，Dr. Chung成為南加州第一位華裔女醫師。四百六十五位美國國最優秀的飛行員敬她為母親。

Photo courtesy of Los Angeles Examiner and California Historical Society Title Insurance and Trust Photo Collection. Department of Special Collections, University of Southern California.

U.S. Navy crew during World War II.
(Chow Hoy, the only Chinese
member, is in the center.)

二次大戰期間的美國海軍。（圖中
的 Chow Hoy 是唯一的華人）

Photo courtesy of Chinese Historical
Society of Southern California

Captain Victor Quon worked for
McGregor Radio Studios in 1943. Later,
he became a music director for CBS.

一九四三年，Victor Quon上尉在
McGregor電台工作。他後來出任哥
倫比亞廣播公司的音樂總監。

Photo courtesy of Chinese Historical
Society of Southern California

Los Angeles neighborhood buddies met by chance after the war in Nice, France, in 1945. Left to Right : Roy Fong of the 9th Air Force, Lee Chin with Patton's 3rd Army and Jimmy Woo, paratrooper with the 82nd Airborne Division.

一九四五年，住在洛杉磯的左右鄰居們為了作戰，在法國尼斯的戰場上不期而遇，空軍第九師的Roy Fong，。陸軍第三師的Lee Chin和第八十二空軍團分部的傘兵Jimmy Woo。

Photo courtesy of Jim Fong

寂寞的辮子

Howard Yip went to work daily with the sign shown above displayed on his back - a notice to fellow workers that he is Chinese and anxious to help smash the Japanese.

Howard Yip 每天上工，背上有特別標誌，向同胞
表示他是華人，並要支持他們擊潰日軍。

Photo courtesy of Los Angeles Examiner and California Historical Society Title Insurance and Trust Photo Collection. Department of Special Collections, University of Southern California.

Miss Ethel Mildred Lee, 25, was a Chinese worker at Calship in the 1940s. She helped build the S.S. China Victory, the first ship to be constructed at the plant

一九四零年代，二十五歲的Ethel Mildred
Lee在加州船塢工作，她幫忙打造製作第一
艘船—S.S.中國勝利號。

Photo courtesy of Los Angeles Examiner and California Historical Society Title Insurance and Trust Photo Collection. Department of Special Collections, University of Southern California.

### ▶ Demolition of China City

In 1949 another disastrous fire demolished the main section of China City. The remainder of Old Chinatown was almost completely torn down for the construction of the Hollywood/Santa Ana Freeway. The last tenant left the Garnier Building in 1953, and most of the Chinese civic organizations and institutions moved to the greater new Chinatown area.

### 拆毀中國市

一九四九年，中國市的主要地段又發生了嚴重大火，鄰近好萊塢和聖塔安納公路邊，僅餘的舊城部分幾乎燃燒殆盡，最後一家租戶於一九五三年搬離加尼爾樓，市民組織和公司也大多搬到新中國城。

The "Los Angeles Chinese", an evacuation plane, 1945.

一九四五年，第一架驅逐機 ─「洛杉磯華人」號。

Photo courtesy of The You Chung Hong and Mabel Chin Hong Archives

寂寞的辮子

The Chinese Student Club of USC in mid-1940s. The American-born Chinese men and women searched for their own places in both their Chinese and American worlds. They became Americanized, adopting the fashions and interests typical of their generation.

一九四零年代中期南加大的華裔學生。在美出生的華裔子弟努力為自己在美國人和華人的圈子裡找尋一席之地。他們最終還是美國化了，適應本地和屬於新一代的流行和嗜好。

**Photo courtesy of S.P. Lee Photo Collection**

The last block of Old Chinatown along Los Angeles Street, circa 1946.

一九四六年，華埠沿著洛杉磯街的最後一段。

Photo courtesy of Johnny Yee.

San Pedro Street City Market, 1947.

一九四七年，市集的聖彼卓街。

**Photo courtesy of The City Market of Los Angeles**

寂寞的辮子

"Stags" basketball team members with friends showcased awards at the Poly High School in 1949. Left to right: Roy Bague, Jim Fong, Lily Dong, Joyce Bague, Lincoln Ong, Wayne Chan, unknown, Eleanor Bague, and Don Fung.

一九四九年， Stags 籃球隊的隊員和友人們勝利後在Poly高中留影。由左至右：Roy Bague、Jim Fong、Lily Dong、Joyce Bague、Lincoln Ong、Wayne Chan、不知名、Eleanor Bague和Don Fung。

Photo courtesy of Jim Fong

The Los Angeles "Mandarin" and Arizona "Sino Amerians" softball teams in 1948.

一九四八年，洛杉磯的Mandarin和Sino American壘球隊。

Photo courtesy of Jim Fong

寂寞的辮子

"Guardsmen" athletic club in the Adams and SanPedro Streets area, circa 1940.

一九四零年，在亞凱街和聖彼卓街一帶的 Guardsmen運動俱樂部。

Photo courtesy of S.P. Lee Photo Collection

Noel Toy (Ngun Yee Toy) showcased her talents as a performer in Broadway revues and as the top Chinese fan dancer in San Francisco's Forbidden City, a popular night club in the 1940's. In 1939, Toy was a great supporter of Los Angeles' China Relief Fund. Her theatrical and acting career in Los Angeles continued for several decades. Currently, Toy is the president of the China Society, a Southern California organization dedicated to the better understanding of the Chinese history and culture.

彩銀意在百老匯劇中表現個人才藝，她也是一九四零年代受歡迎的夜總會–San Francisco's Forbidden City的頂尖舞者。一九三九年彩銀意大力支持洛杉磯地區的援助中國運動，彩銀意的戲劇表演事業在洛杉磯地區持續了數十年，目前，她是南加中國協會的主席，該會致力推廣中美歷史文化交流。

Photo courtesy of Noel Toy

Mr. Wilbur Woo, at the time an Examiner in the Office of Postal Censorship, was inspecting mails for secret messages and codes during World War II. In 1945, Woo became the Chief of the Technical Operations Division in its Southern California District Office.

一九四五年，二次大戰期間，在郵局稽查處擔任檢查員的胡國棟正在檢視機密文件和密碼。他後來升任南加地區營運部的最高主管。

Photo courtesy of Wilbur Woo

In the Los Angeles Chinatown Rice Bowl parade, women carried the China national flag, into which bystanders threw money to raise funds for the war relief effort in China.

女士們執旗在洛杉磯華埠的飯碗遊行前進，爲中國戰後重建募款。

Photo courtesy of Wilbur Woo

Chinese Boy Scout Troop 718 with Peter Soo Hoo, Jr., Andrew Chin, Donald Chang and Nowland C. Hong (center) at Y.C. Hong's residence, the early 1940s.

一九四零年早期，華裔童軍團七一八小隊和Peter Soo Hoo, Jr. ，Andrew Chin, Donald Chang和Nowland C. Hong（中）在Y.C. Hong的家裡。

Photo courtesy of The You Chung Hong and Mabel Chin Hong Archives

寂寞的辮子

The American Women's Voluntary Services at the New Chinatown Canteen. The center was designed to assist with various war relief programs and to be a "home away from home" for American and Chinese servicemen, circa 1944-46.

一九四四年到四六年新中國城Canteen的美國
婦女志願服務團，協助戰爭救援，是美軍和
華裔軍人之家。

Photo courtesy of The You Chung Hong and Mabel Chin Hong Archives

# *Chapter 6*

## *Postwar Years in New Chinatown*
## 戰後的新中國城

"Chien Hua" softball group at the El Sereno playground, circa 1947-48. Front row, left to right: Eugene Hoo, Stephen Yee, Lee Leong, Stanley Quon, George Wong. Back row, left to right: Albert Lee, Dan Wong, James Chu, unknown, unknown, and Frank Quon.

一九四七到四八年，在El Sereno遊樂場上運動的華裔
壘球隊，後排左至右：Eugene Hoo、Stephen Yee、Lee
Leong、 Stanley Quon、 George Wong，前排左至右：
Albert Lee、Dan Wong、James Chu、不知名、不知名
和Frank Quon。

Photo courtesy of Earl Hing

## The 1950s

By 1950, there were 110 groceries, 350 laundries and 180 restaurants supporting a community largely through outside patronage. The Chinese population in the Los Angeles County nearly doubled from 5,330 in 1940 to 9,187 in 1950. In 1952, the McCarran-Walter Act made all races eligible for naturalization and eliminated race as a bar to immigration. By the mid-1950s, more than half of the Chinese population was native born. Later in the decade, restrictive covenants on the use and ownership of property were removed. Laws such as the Refugee Relief Act of 1953 and the Refugee Escape Act of 1957 and 1959 also benefited Chinese immigrants.

The population of Chinese women in particular increased rapidly after World War II. In 1950, almost 40 percent of the Chinese population in Los Angeles were women. This was largely due to the War Brides Act of 1945 and 1946 Fiancees Act which permitted the entry of alien spouses and minor dependents of members of U.S. armed forces. There was also a dramatic increase in American-born children of second and third generations. The increase of the female Chinese population in Los Angeles led to an increased emphasis on family life.[1]

The favorable attitude in America toward China and Chinese Americans grew stronger after World War II. Chinese were finally able to become naturalized citizens, intermarry with whites in California, own land, and find work and housing outside the boundaries of Chinatown. Chinese people were becoming increasingly middle class, and striving for assimilation into American society.

Chinese communities were becoming more and more Americanized and active in politics. Chinese-American youths and adults joined American clubs such as Little League, Boy and Girls Scouts, Brownies, Los Angeles Women's Club, Y.W.C.A., Y.M.C.A. and Kiwanis Club.

## 一九五零年代

到一九五零年時，來自社區外四面八方的遊客，惠顧支持華人經營的一百一十家雜貨店、三百五十家洗衣店和一百八十家餐館。洛杉磯縣的華裔人口從一九四零年代的五千三百三十人，在往後的十年間幾乎加倍成長，一九五零年已達九千一百八十七人。一九五二年，麥卡倫－華特法案使各族裔都可歸化入籍，解除了移民的族裔限制。到一九五零年代中期，半數以上的華人都是在本地出生，五零年代末，地產使用和擁有的限制條例也被廢除，一九五三年的援助難民法案、一九五七年和一九五九年的難民逃離法案，也裨益華人良多。

二次大戰後，華裔婦女人數明顯增加，一九五零年，洛杉磯百分之四十的華人是女性。一九四五年的戰爭新娘法案和一九四六年的未婚妻法案允許軍人的配偶和未成年子女來美團聚，戰後在美出生的第二代和第三代兒童也明顯增加，洛杉磯華裔女性人數增加使得家庭生活日形重要。[1]

美國人在二次大戰期間衍生對中國和華人的好感仍在，華人終於可入籍成爲公民，在加州與白人結婚、擁有地產，在中國城外居住和謀生，華人逐漸步入中產階級，走出中國城，努力融入美國社會。

華人社區日漸美國化，政治活動也愈趨熱絡。大多數的華人青少年和成人都加入美國組織，如少棒隊、男女童軍、女童軍、洛杉磯婦女會、青年會、女青年會和同濟會等。

Howard Jong, a pioneering Chinese-American aeronautics engineer, caught 16 fish at Pierpoint Landing in Long Beach, circa 1950.

一九五零年，華裔航空工程師 Howard Jong在長堤的Pierpoint Landing捕了十六條魚。

Photo courtesy of Howard Jong

The Lonely Queue

## ▶ Chinese Confucius Temple

Recognizing the increasing need to promote Chinese language, art and culture, the Chinese community raised a total of $60,000 to help build the Chinese Confucius Temple (CCT) in 1952. On May 18, 1952, the CCT held its first Chinese language classes with an enrollment of 60 in the heart of Chinatown. The CCT was founded by the Chinese Consolidated Benevolent Association with the support of its 27 district and fraternal family associations.

Today, the CCT operates seven days a week with classes from kindergarten to 9th grade. Afternoon classes are held Monday to Friday, and full day classes on Saturday and Sunday. Today, the CCT is one of the largest Chinese schools in Southern California with more than 1,000 students of Chinese ancestry.

### 中華孔廟

有感於提倡中國語言、藝術和文化的需要，一九五二年，華人社區籌集了六萬元興建中華孔廟。一九五二年五月十八日，中華孔廟在中國城中心開辦了第一個中文班，共有六十人上課，由中華會館和旗下二十七個宗親會所贊助經費。

中華孔廟每週七天上課，由幼稚班到九年級，下午班每週一至週五上課，週六和週日有全天課。中華孔廟是目前南加州最大的中文學校，有一千多名華裔學生。

The swearing in of Judge Delbert Wong at the Los Angeles Municipal Court on Jan. 30, 1959.
As the first Chinese American appointed as judge in the continental United States, the appointment was recognized as an historic event and received national media attention.

一九五九年一月三十日，黃錦紹法官在洛杉磯市政法庭宣誓就任。他是美國本土內第一位華裔法官，這項任命成為歷史紀錄，備受全國媒體的矚目。

Photo courtesy of Judge Delbert Wong and Dolores Wong

### Los Angeles Chinese Drum and Bugle Corps

The Los Angeles Chinese Drum and Bugle Corps was founded in 1954 with the motto of "One for All and All for One." Composed of boys and girls aged 10 to 21 from the Greater Los Angeles area, its primary objectives were to build strong character; develop good citizenship and promote responsibility; develop pride and loyalty; and promote understanding and harmony between ethnic groups. The corps competed in many drum corps contests throughout the United States during the 50s, 60s and 70s. In 1974, 1975 and 1976 the corps was one of ten finalists in the Drum Corps West contest held in the Pacific Northwest area.[2]

### 洛杉磯華人鼓號樂隊

洛杉磯華人鼓號樂隊於一九五四年成立，以「團結一心」爲信條，號召大洛杉磯地區十到二十一歲男女生參加，以塑造堅毅性格，培育良好公民，加強責任感，養成榮譽和忠心，促進族裔之間的瞭解和諧。在五零、六零和七零年代，樂隊在全美各地參加比賽，一九七四、七五和七六年，並入圍西北太平洋區鼓號樂隊西區競賽決選的十隊之一。[2]

After Tommy Yee served in the Korean War, he returned to Los Angeles where he met his wife, Nancy Yee, in 1954.

一九五四年，Tommy Yee自韓戰歸來，返回洛杉磯與妻子余黃新珠團聚。

Photo courtesy of Nancy Yee

### Chinese Chamber of Commerce of Los Angeles

During the 1950s Chinatown owned and operated more than 110 grocery stores, 350 laundromats, 180 restaurants and two churches supporting a community of about 10,000 people. In 1955, the Chinese Chamber of Commerce of Los Angeles was established by a group of business people to promote and encourage the development of the Chinese-American business community throughout the greater Los Angeles area. Since then, the Chamber has acted as a strong influence for positive action on key legislative and regulatory issues affecting the Chinese community and its businesses. This organization has provided a forum for discussions on issues relevant to both the Chinese and greater Los Angeles business communities.

In addition to serving as an advocate of the Chinese business community, the chamber has promoted cultural awareness to improve inter-ethnic relations by organizing events such as the Chinese New Year Golden Dragon Parade and the Miss Los Angeles Chinatown Pageant.

### 羅省中華總商會

一九五零年代，華埠共有一百一十家雜貨鋪、三百五十家洗衣店、一百八十家餐館和兩所教會，社區共有約一萬人。一九五五年，一些商人們為促進華商的發展和繁榮，發起成立羅省中華總商會。自此，商會在推動對華人社區和華商有正面影響的關鍵立法議題上，極具影響力，商會同時提供了討論與華人和洛杉磯商業有關議題的平台。

除了領導華商維護爭取權益，商會也舉辦如中國新年金龍遊行、華埠小姐選美等活動，以提倡文化認知，並促進族裔和諧。

The Los Angeles Chinatown Optimist Club welcomed Judge Delbert Wong in 1959.

一九五九年，洛杉磯中國城樂觀者俱樂部歡迎黃錦紹法官。

Photo courtesy of Judge Delbert Wong and Dolores Wong

Y.C. Hong (front row, 1st left) and Mabel Hong (2nd row, 2nd right) joined members of Los Angeles' Chinese community in welcoming Senator Hiram Fong at the Hong Kong Restaurant in New Chinatown, circa 1959.

一九五九年，洪耀宗（前排左一）和Mabel Hong（二排右二）在中國城香港餐廳和社區一起歡迎參議員Hiram Fong。

Photo courtesy of The You Chung Hong and Mabel Chin Hong Archives

Chinese Golf Club members received awards in its annual golf tournament at the Montebello Country Club, circa early 1950s.

一九五零年代早期，華裔高球俱樂部在蒙地貝婁高爾夫球場舉行第一屆高球賽的頒獎典禮。

Photo courtesy of Wilbur Woo

寂寞的辮子

Chinese language school students
before graduation, 1959

一九五九年中文學校的畢業典禮。

Photo courtesy of the Shades of Los
Angeles Archives/Los Angeles
Public Library

David Lee (back row, 2nd from left) and his
family members in front of Man Jen Low.  It
was known as General Lee's Restaurant, and
became the most popular Chinese restaurant
in Los Angeles in the early 1950s. It received
many culinary awards and attracted local
celebrities and dignitaries.

David Lee（後排左二）和家人在萬珍樓前。
一九五零年代，萬珍樓改名李上校餐館，成
為洛杉磯最受歡迎的餐館，獲得無數美食獎，
社區名流經常惠顧。

Photo courtesy of David and Yuki Lee

### ▶ Pioneering Chinese Business Woman

Mrs. Grace Wong Chow entered the insurance field in 1941. Eight years later, she became the very first Chinese woman to sell one million dollars of insurance in a year. Thus, she was qualified as a member of the Million Dollar Round Table in 1949. For five consecutive years, she reached the same sales quota of $1 million per year. Chow became the first Chinese woman to qualify for life membership in the prestigious Million Dollar Club of Franklin Life Insurance in 1954. In 1956, she was the only Chinese mentioned in the first edition of "Who's Who in California." Throughout the years, Chow has devoted extensive time and energy to various civic and community services. In 1968, she was the first Chinese woman appointed to serve as a member of the Commission on Human Relations for the City of Los Angeles. And she was a co-founder of the First Chinese Baptist Church. [3]

### 華商婦女先驅

Grace Wong Chow在一九四一年投入保險業，八年後，即成爲全美第一位華裔女性年度百萬經紀。一九四九年，她入選百萬經紀圓桌會員，連續五年都達到百萬業績。一九五四年，她成爲第一位獲得法蘭克林保險百萬經紀俱樂部終生會員殊榮，一九五六年，又是列名加州名人榜的唯一華裔女性。多年來，她在社區服務和工作上，投入了大量時間和精力，一九六八年，她是第一位被指派擔任洛市人際關係委員會委員的華裔女性，她同時也是第一華人浸信會的創辦人之一。[3]

Tommy Yee, owner of the Moon Plaza Restaurant on San Pedro Street, 1956.

一九五六年，Moon Plaza餐館的業主Tommy Yee在聖彼卓街上。

Photo courtesy of Nancy Yee.

Thomas Hom (far left) with sons Gordon and Gilbert, along with other family members on the docks in San Pedro Harbor, bidding farewell to their father/grandfather, who worked as a chef on the American President Lines in 1955.

一九五五年・Thomas Hom（前排左一）和其子Gordon、Gilbert Hom為在聖彼卓碼頭American President Line工作的父親/祖父送行。

Photo courtesy of S.P. Lee Family Collection.

### First Chinese Baptist Church

Founded in 1952, the First Chinese Baptist Church offered its services to the Chinatown community in a vacant noodle factory on Hill Street. Rev. Thomas Lowe led the church in the first sanctuary in 1957.[4] It has grown from nine members to its current congregation of 2,000, predominantly Chinese Americans. The church's programs include daily Bible teaching, training in ministry skills, music, sports and fellowship. Today, many Chinese Americans come from distant suburbs to attend one of three Sunday services, conducted in English and Cantonese. A new 1,000-seat sanctuary and a multi-purpose gym are under construction.

### 第一華人浸信會

第一華人浸信會成立於一九五二年，教會最初在Hill街上一處空置的麵廠做禮拜，一九五七年，Thomas Lowe牧師領導會眾建立了第一所教堂。[4] 教會已從昔日的九名教友增加到今日的二千人，大多數的教友是華人。教會提供的節目和活動有查經、傳道研習、音樂、體育和召募等。現在，有很多來自各地的華人參加教會以英語和粵語進行的主日禮拜，教會目前正在興建可容納一千人的教堂和一多用途的體育館。

Jeff Chan, a long-time Los
Angeles resident, was crowned
"Mr. Chinatown USA" in San
Francisco in 1958.
Photo courtesy of Jeff Chan.

一九五八年，久居洛杉磯的Jeff
Chan在舊金山接受「美國華埠先
生」獎。

Photo courtesy of Jeff Chan.

寂寞的辮子

811 Signal Service battalion at the Fort
McArthur in San Pedro in 1951. Members
Jim Fong (back row, 3rd left), and Clifford
Chan (2nd row, 4th right) are the only
Chinese Americans in the group.

一九五一年，在聖彼卓的Fort McArthur陸
軍基地的八一一軍團軍官，Jim Fong（後
排左三）和Clifford Chan（二排右四）是
隊中僅有的華裔。

Photo courtesy of Jim Fong

Owner Benny Eng (1st from left) and Chef Benny
Ong (2nd from left) at the Wan-Q Restaurant on
Pico Boulevard in West Los Angeles, circa 1950s.

一九五零年代，西洛杉磯Pico Boulevard的Wan-Q
餐廳業主Benny Eng（前排左）和大廚Benny Ong
（二排左）。

Photo courtesy of Mei Ong.

Charles and Mary Louie at their family-run
Lim Sing Laundry on 8637 Pico Boulevard
in West Los Angeles. They served mostly the
Jewish community for more than 20 years,
circa 1950s. Their children helped laundering
and ironing more than 100 garments each day
for 22 cents a piece. The Louies, like many
other Chinese laundries, lived and worked on
the premises.

洗衣店服務猶太社區逾二十年，孩子們每日洗
熨一百多件衣裳，每件兩毛兩分，和其他華人
洗衣店一般，一家人工作和居住都在店裡。

Photo courtesy of Mei Ong.

Mei Git Tuey (2nd row, 1st from left), an active member in the local Chinese community, with her family members in front of their house in South Central area, circa 1955.

一九五五年，華裔社區活躍人士 Mei Git Tuey（二排左一）和家人 在洛市中南區的家宅前。

Photo courtesy of Mei Ong.

# *Chapter 7*

*Chinatown Troubles*
紛擾的中國城

Banquet at the Chinese Presbyterian
Church, 1950.

一九五零年，華人長老會的餐會。

Photo courtesy of the Shades of Los
Angeles Archives/Los Angeles
Public Library

### The 1960s Immigration Reform

In 1960, the Chinese population reached 19,286 in Los Angeles County. In 1967, an estimated 3,500 immigrants arrived in Los Angeles. Chinatown continued to be the main business district, residential area and the center of the Chinese community. The City of Monterey Park in San Gabriel Valley, the largest Chinese concentration outside the City of Los Angeles, had only 346 Chinese residents.

In October 1965, President Lyndon Johnson signed an act that abolished the national origins immigration quota system. It was the first real immigration reform in over a century. The new immigration law set a new quota of 20,000 persons from any country regardless of racial or ethnic origin. The resulting new wave of Asian immigrants came from Hong Kong, Taiwan, Vietnam, Burma, Thailand, and Singapore, and helped diversify the Chinese community. Because the new immigrants tended to come from urban rather than rural areas, some were affluent, well educated, and already spoke some English when they came to the U.S.

Chinatown was not sufficiently equipped to cope with the problems and conditions created by such a large influx of new immigrants to the Los Angeles area. The increased immigration exacerbated growing problems of substandard housing, under-employment, poor medical care and inadequate social services for the young and old.

### 一九六零年代　移民法變革

一九六零年時，洛縣華裔人口已達一萬九千二百八十六人。一九六七年，估計有三千五百名移民來到洛杉磯，中國城依舊是主要商業區、住宅區和華人社區中心。聖蓋博谷的蒙特利公園市在當時是洛市以外最大的華人社區，但當時也只有三百四十六名華人。

一九六五年十月，詹森總統簽署了一項廢止移民國家配額系統，這是一世紀以來首度真正的移民改革。新移民法規定，不論族裔，每個國家有二萬人的新配額，新移民潮由是而起，來自亞洲各地，包括香港、台灣、越南、緬甸、泰國、新加坡，以及非亞裔國家的新移民，使華人社區更為多元化。這些新移民大多來自都市，而非鄉村地區，有些人受過良好教育，環境富裕，而且在進入美國時就已經能說英語。

大批新移民湧入洛杉磯地區引起的問題使華埠不知所措，如居住品質不佳、失業、衛生和健康情形不良、照顧老幼的社會服務也付之闕如。

## ▶ Chinatown Troubles

The 1960 census showed that one third of the housing in Chinatown was substandard. Of the 1,513 housing units analyzed, 593 were characterized as "deteriorating," 91 as "dilapidated." Overcrowding in Chinatown had also caused housing prices to skyrocket.[1]

In 1968, a study conducted by the Oriental American Survey Project revealed that of 193 surveyed families in Chinatown, 63 percent spoke only Chinese at home, compared to 4 percent in which English was the exclusive language. One-third of the families were surviving on less than $3,000 a year even though the average household income of $10,000 in Chinatown. This poverty resulted in increased gang problems and crime in Chinatown.

### 紛擾的中國城

一九六零年的人口普查顯示，有三分之一以上的華埠住屋不合標準，受檢的一千五百一十三間住房有五百九十三間被評為危樓，九十一間被評為已坍塌，更糟的是，日漸擁擠的華埠使住房的價格飛漲。[1]

一九六八年，一項由亞美民意計劃所做的研究揭露，受訪的華埠一百九十三戶人家中，百分之六十三在家只說中文，百分之四僅說英語；為數達三分之一的家庭每年收入不及三千元，而當時一般家庭的年收入大約是一萬元。貧窮導致幫派事件和犯罪問題的日漸增加。

Former California Governor Ronald Reagan came to Los Angeles Chinatown to garner community support, circa 1960s.

一九六零年代，前加州州長雷根前來洛市拜訪，爭取社區的支持。

Photo courtesy of The You Chung Hong and Mabel Chin Hong Archives

Wally Quon (center) with Mama Quon at the Grand Star Restaurant in 1965. For nearly 50 years the Quon family has catered to lunch crowds at the Grand Star Restaurant.

一九六五年，Wally Quon（中）和其母在Grand Star餐館。五十多年來，Quon家在Grand Star餐館以中國菜款待了無數非華裔的友人。

Photo courtesy of Wally Quon

寂寞的辮子

Sanora Wong Howe, Beulah Quo (actress) and James Wong Howe at the Quon Bros Grand Star Restaurant, circa 1960. James W. Howe was an Oscar winning Chinese-American cinematographer shooting more than 125 films over 60 some years.

一九六零年，Sanora Wong Howe，郭鄧如鶯（演員）和James Wong Howe在Quon Bro's Grand Star餐廳合影，James Wong Howe是華裔奧斯卡獎攝影師，六十多年來拍了一百二十五部影片。

Photo courtesy of Wally Quon

Cathay Bank, the first Chinese-American bank in Southern California, opened its storefront office in 1962 to promote the economic development of the Los Angeles Chinatown community. Today, Cathay Bank is ranked as the 5th largest commercial bank in Los Angeles County.

南加州第一家華資銀行—國泰銀行於一九六二年開業，促進洛市華埠社區的經濟發展，今日，國泰銀行已是洛縣第五大商業銀行。

Photo courtesy of Cathay Bank

Cathay Bank President George Ching (2nd from right) at a public service program sponsored by Cathay Bank on August 12, 1962.

一九六二年八月十二日，國泰銀行的第一位總裁程達民（右二）攝於該行贊助的一項社區服務計劃。

Photo courtesy of Cathay Bank

Chairman and officers of the Chinatown Democratic Club in 1960. From left to right: Evelyn Benson, Lupe Gutierrez, Wellington Kwan, May Louie, unknown, Clara Chin, Calvin Chang, Phoebe Yee, Walter Chung, Dolores Wong, Billy Lew, unknown.

一九六零年，華埠民主俱樂部的會長和理事們，左至右Evelyn Benson, Lupe Gutierrez, Wellington Kwan, May Louie, unknown, Clara Chin, Calvin Chang, Phoebe Yee, Walter Chung, Dolores Wong, Billy Lew, 不知名.

Photo courtesy of Clara Chin.

### ▶ Social Center

Under the leadership of the Chinese Chamber of Commerce, a job training program was developed in the late 1960s to help these new immigrants. To counteract the growing tensions, the Chinatown Service Center was founded in 1971 in a small room of the Chinese United Methodist Church. The center provided a bilingual worker and some volunteers assisting newly arrived Chinese with information, translation and other basic social services. Later, the Chinatown Teen Post was established to provide a wide variety of educational and recreational activities for at-risk youth, as well as counseling and summer jobs.

By the late 1960s there were more than 15 Chinese non-profit organizations and nine churches in the Los Angeles Chinese communities, including the pioneering Chinese Presbyterian Church at 2500 Griffin Avenue and the Chinese Congregational Church at 734 E. 9th Place.

Chinatown maintained its role as a social and cultural center. It continued to be the home of many Chinese fraternal groups and the Chinese Consolidated Benevolent Association (CCBA). The CCBA was composed of representatives from 36 fraternal associations. It raised funds for charities and the three Chinese schools in the greater Los Angeles area.

### 社會中心

在羅省中華總商會的倡議領導下，在一九六零年後期舉辦就職訓練以協助新移民謀生。為了紓解當時社區的緊張情勢，一九七一年，華埠服務中心就在華人聯合浸信會的一間小房間裡開始為華人服務。中心有雙語人員和義工協助新移民，提供社區資訊、翻譯和其他基本的社會服務。不多時，華埠青少年輔導計劃也針對行為有偏差的青少年，提供各式教育和娛樂活動，以及家庭計劃和輔導。

一九六零年後期，華埠已有超過十五家非營利機構和九間教會，包括位於2500 Griffin Avenue的華人長老會，和位於734 E. 9th Place的華人公理會。

華埠仍是華人社會的社交和文化中心，即使對已有意遷向郊區的華人亦然，華埠是許多華人宗親組織和中華會館的家。中華會館由三十六所宗親會的代表組成，籌款贊助慈善機構和區內的三所中文學校。

## ▶ New Chinatown Democratic Club

The first Chinese American political club in support of mainstream, national political parties, the Chinatown Democratic Club (CDC), was formed in 1960 by a group of concerned citizens. The club, which was comprised mostly of Chinese Americans, endorsed candidates and raised funds for many political causes such as the Fair Housing Bill. A member of the CDC, Judge Delbert Wong, became the first Chinese American in the continental United States to sit on the First Superior Court in 1961.[2]

### 新中國城民主黨俱樂部

一九六零年，有心人士創辦了第一個支持主流社會全國性政黨的華人組織—華埠民主黨俱樂部。俱樂部成員多為華人，他們支持候選人，為政治活動募款，如支持平等住屋法案，提倡華人參政。黃錦紹法官在一九六一年，成為美國第一位華人法官，執掌第一最高法院。[2]

Benny S. Ong, owner of Canton Chef Restaurant, opened one of the first Chinese fast food restaurants on Pico Boulevard in West Los Angeles in 1960. Benny's gourmet Chinese cuisine and special fried egg roll drew many non-Chinese residents in the neighborhood to the restaurant.

一九六零年代，Canton Chef餐館業主Benny S. Ong在西洛杉磯Pico Boulevard開設第一家中式速食店，Benny餐館的美食和可口春捲吸引了附近社區無數非華裔居民的惠顧

Photo courtesy of Mei Ong.

Ada Chan Wong, the 2000 president of the Chinese Chamber of Commerce of Los Angeles with her family members in Los Angeles in 1969. From left to right: Ada, Chris, Catherine (Mother), Wander, Berda and Baldwin.

羅省中華總商會二千年主席黃陳潔嫻於一九六九年與家人攝於洛杉磯。由左至右：陳潔嫻、Chris、Catherine（其母）、Wander、Berda和Baldwin。

Photo courtesy of Ada Chan Wong and Berda Soo-Hoo.

### ▶ Cathay Bank

Though discrimination against Chinese Americans was slowly declining, obtaining housing in a non-Chinese area or getting a loan from a bank continued to be almost impossible for relatively new immigrants. In 1962, Cathay Bank, the first Chinese-American bank in Southern California, was founded to provide financial services and promote the economic development of the Chinese community. With the establishment of Cathay Bank, the community had a financial institution to assist its Chinese-American constituents to own homes and start new businesses. In the late 1960s, many Chinese Americans were then able to move out of Chinatown to live and establish businesses in newer and better neighborhoods throughout Southern California, primarily in the San Gabriel Valley, Eagle Rock, South Bay and Orange County areas. Today, Cathay Bank has expanded to 18 offices throughout California, two offices in New York, and one loan production office in Houston. With assets over $2 billion, Cathay Bank is ranked as the fifth largest commercial bank in Los Angeles County.

### 國泰銀行

儘管對華人的歧視已逐漸淡化，但新移民在非華人區擁有房產或向銀行貸款仍近乎不可能。一九六二年，南加州第一家華資銀行—國泰銀行成立，提供金融服務，並促進華人社區的經濟發展。自此，國泰銀行協助社區華人置產和創業。一九六零年代後期，許多華人遷出華埠，在南加州其他新開發的社區定居或創業，主要集中在聖蓋博谷、鷹石、南灣、和橙縣一帶。至一九九零年代後期，國泰銀行在加州已有十八間分行，在紐約也有二間分行，資產超過二十億元，在洛縣排名第五大商業銀行。

Mrs. Yee Ha Kwong ( 2nd from the right), one of the first Chinese restaurant owners in Beverly Hills, with family members in Chinatown in 1969. Her "Universal Restaurant" was located at La Cienega and Pico Boulevard in 1950

一九六九年，比佛利山第一位華裔餐館業者Yee Ha Kwong（右二）和他的家人們在中國城。一九五零年，他的Universal Restaurant位在La Cienega 和Pico Blvd的交口處。

Photo courtesy of Yee Ha Kwong.

# *Chapter 8*

*The Development of Suburban Chinatown*
華埠近郊的發展

## ► The 1970s   Open Immigration

During the early 1970s, a growing number of Southeast Asian immigrants and refugees arrived. Many were from Hong Kong, Taiwan, China and Vietnam, and settled in Chinatown as their entry community to avoid language and cultural barriers. Many affluent Chinese moved to the suburban areas of the San Gabriel Valley, Rancho Palos Verdes, Cerritos, Garden Grove, Anaheim, Huntington Beach and Irvine.

Between 1970 and 1980, the population of Chinatown continued to grow, from 5839 to 8652. The average household size was 3.4 people with an annual household income below $15,000, compared to the citywide figure of $18,000. Without government subsidized housing programs, many people lived in cubicles, illegally subdivided units.  Others would sublease one bedroom of their two-bedroom apartment to another family. About half of all the Chinatown apartment buildings were more than 50 years old and in need of repair; 24 percent lacked kitchen facilities and 21 percent lacked plumbing. Overcrowding was four times the citywide rate.[1]

Chinatown leaders organized to demand their fair share of social and educational services from the local government.  Their advocacy worked to establish the Chinatown Service Center, Chinatown Senior Citizens Center, Friends of the Chinatown Library, Teen Post, new churches and temples, and many other socially oriented entities. Chinatown continued to serve as the Chinese cultural center of Southern California, and was home to more than 28 benevolent associations.

Among these social service groups, the Chinatown Service Center (CSC) is a cornerstone organization providing child and family support services in the Chinese-American community. Its services include a family health clinic, employment training, social services information, child abuse prevention and counseling services for at-risk children and youth, parenting training, and domestic violence treatment services. It has offices in Chinatown and Monterey Park serving clients throughout the Los Angeles County.

Chinatown also functioned as a regional retail and trade center. Major economic activities were centered around retail stores, banking, tourism, the restaurant trade, garment manufacturing and the food processing/packaging businesses.  The construction of Mandarin Plaza on North Broadway represented the first significant development in the area in over 20 years and heralded a new era of commercial expansion in Chinatown.

Changes in Chinatown were also reflected by the growing number of new Vietnamese-Chinese-owned shops and restaurants along North Spring, Broadway and Hill Streets. Many of Chinatown's businesses were owned by the Vietnamese Chinese. There was tension between the more established Chinese business owners and those from Vietnam who were a mixture of ethnic Chinese and ethnic Vietnamese.

## 一九七零年代 開放移民

一九七零年代初期，東南亞的新移民和難民陸續抵達華埠，其中多來自香港、台灣、中國大陸和越南，他們將華埠視為來美第一站，選擇在此定居，以避免語言和文化隔閡的不便。較富裕者則在聖蓋博谷、帕樂斯福德莊、喜瑞都、園林、安納罕、杭廷頓海灘、爾灣等地定居和就業。

一九七零至一九八零年，華埠人口持續增加，在缺乏政府住房補助計劃的情形下，人口總數由五千八百三十九人增加至八千六百五十二人，平均每一住戶有三點四個人，年收入不及一萬五千元，當時城裡家庭平均收入為一萬八千元。由於住房不敷所需，許多人住在非法隔間的斗室裡，有的則向兩房公寓的人家分租一間房，大約有半數的華埠公寓樓房都超過五十年，亟待整修，其中百分之二十四沒有廚房，百分之二十一沒有排水設施，擁擠程度是全市的四倍。[1]

社區領袖聯合向地方政府要求亟需的平等的社會和教育服務，在他們的倡議和努力下，成立了華埠服務中心、華埠老人中心、華埠圖書館之友會、Teen Post，教會和寺廟，及以提供社會服務為主旨的組織，以補傳統性團體的不足。華埠仍然是南加州華人的文化中心，也是超過二十八大宗親團體的家。

華埠服務中心是主要的社服組織，提供華裔社區家庭和兒童所需的服務，包括家庭健康診療、就職訓練、社會服務諮商、預防虐待兒童、青少年輔導、親職教育和家庭暴力防範等。華埠服務中心在華埠和蒙市設有服務處，服務對象遍及洛縣各地。

華埠也是區域零售和商業中心，城裡的零售店、金融業、觀光業、餐館、車衣製造、食品加工和包裝業，帶來了蓬勃的商業活動。北百老匯街Mandarin Plaza的興建是華埠二十餘年來最具規模的商業建設，引領華埠走入商業發展的另一紀元。

沿著北士丙令街、百老匯街和曉街，越華經營的商家和餐館日漸增加，也反映著華埠的演變，許多華埠的業者是**越華裔**。華裔業主與來自越南的越華裔業主之間的關係一度緊張。

寂寞的辮子

## ▶ The Birth of Suburban Chinatown

In the mid-1970s, many Chinese Americans moved to Monterey Park. Most were young professionals or established families from the Chinatown, the City Market and the San Pedro Street neighborhoods. The Chinese population in Monterey Park reached 2,200 in 1970, an increase of 536 percent in 10 years, and outnumbered the surrounding Chinese communities in the San Gabriel Valley.

By the late 1970s, with political unrest in Asia, overseas Chinese interest in Monterey Park grew, causing property values to skyrocket. A major influence on the large influx of Chinese to the community was Frederic Hsieh. For several years, he had not only been buying property in Monterey Park, but aggressively promoting the city as the "Chinese Beverly Hills" in Chinese language newspapers throughout Hong Kong and Taiwan. In his ad, Hsieh pointed out the presence of good schools, affordable housing, green parks and the proximity to downtown Los Angeles. As a result, Taiwanese and Hong Kong immigrants were drawn to Monterey Park in the 1970's. Monterey Park was functioning as a new Chinese community with large clusters of Chinese residents and various kinds of Chinese businesses. [2]

By the end of the decade, the number of Chinese residents in Monterey Park (8,082) would compose 30.8 percent of the entire Chinese population in the cities of the San Gabriel Valley. Monterey Park's median family income would grow to $22,568, as compared with the Los Angeles County figure of $17,563. The ethnic breakdown of income for the city shows an even wider disparity: for whites, $28,242; blacks, $16,364; Hispanics, $21,595; Asians, $30,119. [3]

The area would continue to grow. Ten years later, in 1990, the City of Monterey Park's Annual Financial Report would show that the combined deposits in Monterey Park's 26 financial institutions had grown to over $1.9 billion, or roughly $30,000 for every man, woman and child in town. Chinese banking institution experienced a tremendous growth with the number of bank offices increasing from 3 in 1970 to 130 in 1989. [4]

## 華埠郊區的形成

一九七零年年中，許多專業人士或經濟情況較好的家庭，搬離華埠、市集、和聖彼卓社區，遷至蒙特利公園市。一九七零年，蒙特利公園市的華裔人口達二千二百人，較十年前增加百分之五百三十六，成長率超過鄰近的華裔社區。

一九七零年代後期，由於亞洲地區的政局不安，海外華人遷居蒙特利公園市的興趣大增，使得地價飆升。謝叔綱對華人移民的擁入有極重大的影響，數年之間，他不僅收購蒙特利公園房地產，更在香港和台灣的許多華文報紙上積極促銷，強調區好、價格合理，緊鄰洛市、有綠地，將蒙特利公園塑造成華人的比佛利山，結果吸引了大批港台新移民前來此地。他在廣告中指出，蒙市擁有好學區、房價合適，又近洛杉磯城中區，以此吸引來大批港台新移民。結果，蒙特利公園市成了華人聚居和華商經營生意的新華人社區。[2]

一九七零年代末，蒙市的華裔居民（八千零八十二人）已佔聖蓋博谷各城市華裔人口總數的百分之三十點八。相對於洛縣平均家庭收入的一萬七千五百六十三元，蒙市的平均家庭收入增加至二萬二千五百六十八元，族裔間的收入差距明顯：白人家庭為二萬八千二百四十二元、黑人家庭為一萬六千三百六十四元、西裔家庭為二萬一千五百九十五元、亞裔家庭為三萬零一百一十九元。[3]

區域發展持續進行，十年後的一九九零年，蒙市年度財務報告顯示，蒙市二十六家金融機構的總存款超過十九億元，大約是城裡一男一女再加一個孩子即有三萬元的儲蓄。華資銀行界也經歷了大幅成長，從一九七零年的三間分行到一九八九年的一百三十間分行。[4]

California Secretary of State March Fong Eu and Chinese Historical Society of Southern California President Chuck Yee re-enact the driving of the Golden Spike, at the Golden Spike Centennial Celebration at Lang Station on September 5, 1976. The event was to commemorate the thousands of Chinese laborers who worked so diligently to complete San Fernando Tunnel, linking the southern and northern portions of the Southern Pacific Railroad at Lang Station on September 5, 1876.

一九七六年九月五日，加州州務卿余江月桂與南加州華人歷史學會會長Chuck Yee在Lang Station的金釘百年紀念會上重新釘下金釘。紀念會在表彰數千華工戮力完成聖弗南度隧道，於一八七六年九月五日在Lang Station連結南太平洋鐵路的南段和北段。

Photo courtesy of Mary Yee.

Members of the Los Angeles Yee family pose for a photo at a party celebrating the 89th birthday of the elder Mr. and Mrs. Yee Chaw Lai in 1972. Mr. Yee Chaw Lai's grandfather Yee Kwang Toy was among the Chinese laborers coming to America to help build the Central Pacific Railroad in 1860s. Yee's father Yee Fwee-Wo had operated a laundry in Midland, Pennsylvania for years. From the California gold fields to Pennsylvania and back to Los Angeles in the 1930s, the Yee family saga was broadcast as part of the PBS series, "American Perspective: Another View" on 145 T.V. stations across the nation in 1981.

一九七二年，Yee家在Yee Chaw Lai的八九壽誕中合影。Yee Chaw Lai的曾祖父Yee Kwang Toy是一八六零年代修築中央太平洋鐵路的華工之一。Yee Chaw Lai的父親Yee Fwee在賓州密德蘭經營洗衣店多年。Yee家在一九三零年代由加州金礦場遷去賓州，再又回到洛杉磯，一九八一年，公共電視在全國一百四十五家電視台播出的節目美國面面觀：另一個角度「American Perspective：Another View」中報導Yee家的故事。

Photo courtesy of Johnny Yee.

寂寞的辮子

133

Group of children and adults
from Castelar school on visit to
Sacramento for the
inauguration of Secretary of
State March Fong Eu.

嘉士德樂小學的家長和學生
們北上沙加緬度參加州務卿
余江月桂的就職典禮。

Photo courtesy of the Shades
of Los Angeles Archives/Los
Angeles Public Library

The orginal Castelar School building, which would be demolished in 1973 for not meeting earthquake safety standards. Castelar School is the second oldest continuing school in the district and is the only school with an attached children's center and public library. It has the largest number of Indo-Chinese refugees of any school and had the first Chinese-American elementary school principal in the district.

嘉士德樂小學一九七三年拆除後又重建，以符合防震要求。嘉士德樂小學是學區第二久遠，而且還在授課的校區，也是唯一有幼兒中心，並與公立圖書館相連的學校，學校有學區為數最多的中南半島華裔難民學生，校長也是學區內唯一的華裔校長

Photo courtesy of the Shades of Los Angeles Archives/Los Angeles Public Library

寂寞的辮子

134

March Fong Eu was elected as the first Asian-American Secretary of State in California with a record-setting 3 million votes. In 1994, she was appointed as ambassador to Micronesia.

余江月桂以三百萬選票破紀錄勝選，成為第一位亞裔加州州務卿。一九九四年，她獲派出任密克羅西亞大使。

Photo courtesy of the Shades of Los Angeles Archives/Los Angeles Public Library

## ▶ Vandalism and Harassment

As the Chinese population continued to increase in Monterey Park, strong resentment among long-time, non-Chinese residents of Monterey Park arose. According to some long-time Monterey Park residents, anti-Chinese activity began in the early 1960s. "I had received a call from a non-Chinese Monterey Park resident, threatening my house would be burned down as I was one of the few Chinese moving to the area. Chinese were not welcome at that time.  Police came to my house and patrolled for three to four days," said Wilbur Woo, a current board member of Cathay Bank and a past national president of the Chinese American Citizen Alliance. [5]

By this time, business signs were displayed in Chinese. Chinese was spoken in the streets and Chinese music was piped through speakers in many businesses. Chinese Americans were blamed for the rampant development and subsequent socioeconomic problems in the city, ranging from traffic congestion, rising real estate prices to crime. At one point, Chinese gangs had grown in the city and made headlines in the local newspapers. As a result, some Chinese immigrant children had been subjected to racism in schools. [6]

In September 1980, the Monterey Park Progress announced the addition of its new Chinese language pages as a regular section. Shortly after, the Progress, its sister newspaper, the Alhambra Post-Advocate, and Chinese language theaters in the area were victims of vandalism. A few months later, a fire broke out in one of the offices of the Monterey Park Progress, and the press used to print the Chinese-language section in both papers was destroyed. Though a police investigation later discovered that the fire was accidentally started by some teenagers playing with matches behind the building. However, the Chinese community perceived the incident to be an anti-Chinese backlash.

As a result,  a liberal, multiracial coalition composed of Asian Americans, Latinos and progressive whites called the Coalition for Harmony in Monterey Park (CHAMP) was formed to foster a spirit of citywide harmony and cooperation among the culturally diverse community. And the City Police Department kicked off an "Asian Detail" campaign to educate Chinese merchants about reporting incidents of gang activity. Through these efforts, crime declined in Monterey Park.

## 破壞和勒索

由於中文在蒙市各地四處可見，引起一些居住蒙市多年的非華裔居民的憎恨，一些久居蒙市的居民說，排華活動一九六零年代早期已開始。國泰銀行的董事，也是前同源會全國會長的胡國棟說：「我接到一個蒙市非華裔居民的電話，威脅說我的房子會被放火燒掉，因爲我是搬進這區的少數華人之一，而華人當時是不受歡迎的，警察們來到我家，巡邏了三、四天。」[5]

商家懸掛的招牌是中文，華裔在街頭說中文，很多商家還用播音設備廣播中國音樂。華人被指爲是過度開發和社會問題的罪魁禍首，從交通擁塞、房價飛漲到犯罪事件，都是華人之過。華裔幫派四處作案每每成爲地方報紙的聳動標題，有些華裔學生在學校飽受歧視之苦。[6]

一九八零年九月，蒙市進步報宣佈將定期發行中文版，不多時，該報和其姊妹報—阿罕布拉先鋒郵報都成了受害者，報社被砸，收到仇恨信件，此外，市區的華人戲院入口處也被惡意噴漆、窗戶被砸破。數月之後，蒙市進步報被縱火，印刷兩報中文版面的機器被搗毀。雖然稍後警方的調查發現火災起於意外，是一些少年在樓房後玩火柴所引起，但華人社區咸認這是排華事件。

爲促進族裔和諧，社區人士結合亞裔、西裔和白人的力量，成立蒙市族裔和諧聯盟，倡導多元文化社區的合作與和諧，蒙市市府並鼓勵亞裔商家向警方報告有關幫派的不法活動，在多方配合之下，蒙市的犯罪率漸趨下降。

This traffic light was installed at Bernard and Broadway due to community demand for traffic safety, circa 1970-1972. First row, left to right: Wilbur Woo, community and political activist, Nancy Yee, Sunshine Printing owner, Councilman Gilbert Lindsay and Phoebe Yee.

一九七零到七二年，這個紅綠燈是在社區要求交通安全的情況下，在伯納街和百老匯街的交叉口裝置的。前排左至右：社區和政治活躍人士胡國棟，Sunshing Printing業主余黃新珠，市議員Gilbert Lindsay和Phoebe Yee。

Photo courtesy of Nancy Yee

Nancy Yee, owner of Sunshine Printing and Stationery, opened her store with the first Chinatown Post Office on 982 N. Broadway in New Chinatown in 1972.

Sunshine Printing and Stationary的業主余黃新珠，一九七二年在新中國城內982 N. Broadway開業，華埠的第一間郵局就開在她的店裡。

Photo courtesy of Nancy Yee

From left to right: George Ching, President of Cathay Bank, Sam Yorty, Mayor of City of Los Angeles, Fung Chow Chan, Founder of East West Federal Savings Bank at the East West Federal Savings Bank Grand Opening, in 1972.

左起，一九七二年國泰銀行總裁程達民，洛市市長Sam Yorty，華美聯邦銀行創辦人陳鳳儔在華美聯邦銀行（一九九五年改制為華美銀行）的開幕式上合影。

Photo courtesy of Kelly Chan

Members of the Friends of the Chinatown Library envision an expanded Chinatown Branch Library. Founded in 1977, the Friends of the Chinatown Library is an active group of local friends, parents, business people, school and service workers who help the first Chinatown Library serve an increasing number of new immigrants from Southeast Asia.

華埠圖書館之友會的會員們期待華埠圖書館擴建。一九七七年，社區熱心人士、家長、商業界人士和社會組織為來自東南亞日漸增加的新移民服務，成立華埠圖書館之友會，協助華埠圖書館。

Photo courtesy of the Friends of the Chinatown Library

Betty Tom Chu and Fung Chow Chan, founders of East West Federal Savings Bank, lighting the firecrackers at its first Chinatown office grand opening, in 1972.

譚美生和華美聯邦銀行創辦人陳鳳儔於一九七二年，在華埠該行的第一間，舉行分行的開幕儀式上點燃喜炮。

Photo courtesy of Kelly Chan

寂寞的辮子

138

### ▶ A Prominent Aeronautic Engineer

Howard Jong, a pioneering Chinese-American aeronautics engineer, spent three years in the 1980s improving and maintaining one of the nation's few lightweight surveillance airplanes used by the Monterey Park Police Department for patrol purposes. Today, the Ultralight is on display at the Smithsonian Institute in Washington, D.C. A native Angeleno, Jong graduated from the Curtis Wright Institute in engineering and mechanics in 1936. Since then, he has designed numerous airplane models. He had invented and made improvements to public address, oxygen mask and food service systems, to name a few, when he was an aeronautics engineer for McDonnell Douglas. Today, the Continental Luscombe Association and Howard Jong Air Museum was dedicated to him to recognize his significant contribution to the aerospace industry.[7]

### 傑出航太工程師

華裔航太工程師Howard Jong在一九八零年代期間，費時三年，改進和保養蒙市警察局用於巡邏的輕型偵察機，此類飛機全國已存不多，現有一架輕型飛機陳列在華府史密斯蘇尼恩博物館。Howard Jong在洛杉磯長大，於一九三六年畢業於Curtis Wright學院機械工程系，是麥道飛機公司退休的航空工程師，他的發明和改進成就包括在麥道工程任航太工程師時的Public Address、氧氣罩和食物補給系統。自一九三零年代中期起，他還設計了許多飛機模型，今日的Continental Luscombe協會和Howard Jong航空博物館就是為了紀念他對航太業的貢獻而成立。[7]

Daniel Wong's 1995 calendar showed him bare chested with a gun tucked into his waistband under the words "Promote Peace Not Violence." Dr. Daniel Wong was a former Cerritos mayor and 14-year Cerritos city councilmember. Wong was the first Chinese-American official visiting Premier Li Peng requesting amnesty for protesters at the Tianamen Square crackdown in 1989.

黃錦波赤胸出現在一九九五年的日曆上，腰間別槍，槍上還有「提倡和平非暴力」的字樣。黃錦波是喜瑞都市前市長，曾任該市市議員達十四年，是第一位前去中國會見中國總理李鵬，請求赦免一九八九年天安門事件抗議者的在美華裔民選官員

Photo courtesy of Daniel Wong

Los Angeles Chinese Drum and Bugle
Corps on parade in Glendale.

洛杉磯華人鼓號樂隊在格蘭岱爾遊行。

Photo courtesy of the Shades of Los Angeles
Archives/Los Angeles Public Library.

寂寞的辮子

Mr. Cheng Sai Wong's family pay tribute to
his late wife Fung Lee at the Chung Wah
Chinese Cemetery, 1972.

一九七二年Cheng Sai Wong和家人在中華墓
園追思已逝夫人Fung Lee。

Photo courtesy of Nancy Yee.

# Chapter 9

*The Emergence of the San Gabriel Valley Chinese Communities*
聖蓋博谷華裔社區的掘起

## ▶ The 1980s Chinatown Redevelopment Project

In January of 1980, the Chinatown Redevelopment Project of the Los Angeles City Community Redevelopment Agency (CRA) was adopted, following a couple of years of community discussion and pressure. Its main objective was to provide much needed housing and enhance Chinatown's position as a center of culture and commerce for the Chinese American community. Other important redevelopment goals for the area in the 1980s included promoting the development of local employment opportunities through economic development and private investment and expanding recreational and cultural programs.[1]

Redevelopment brought six low-income housing projects, increased recreational facilities and made civic improvements to the business district. Through its housing assistance program, new Latino and African-American families moved in to the area. Today, most restaurants and shops in Chinatown are patronized frequently by Latinos, African Americans, Whites as well as Chinese residents.

Traffic congestion, housing shortage, and inadequate services have always been important issues in Chinatown. Many residents also were challenged by poor work skills, limited education and low English proficiency. They suffered from poverty, crime, racism, poor health care and isolation from the larger society.

With the influx of Southeast Asian immigrants, Chinatown's traditional economic activities (e.g. retail stores, local tourism, restaurants, garment manufacturing and banking) faced tremendous changes and challenges. With their bilingual and cultural capabilities, many new immigrants engaged in international trade, retail and wholesale, of ethnic consumer products and in various service businesses. Chinatown became more ethnically diverse due to these new resources and markets.[2]

By 1984, half of all Chinatown businesses were owned by the Vietnamese Chinese. Shop signs along streets in Chinatown became trilingual - in Chinese, Vietnamese and English. For example, Asian Tower at the corner of Hill and Ord Streets boasted a clock tower modeled on one in Saigon which was then demolished in the late 1990s. And Wing On Tong, a Chinese herb store dating back more than 90 years to Old Chinatown, displayed its Vietnamese name of Vinh an Duong in its front window. [3]

By the 1980s, Chinatown had expanded in all directions but south: west toward Dodger Stadium, north toward Lincoln Heights and east toward the industrial areas. Over 2.1 million square feet had been redeveloped, mostly for residential purposes. The assessed property valuation had tripled from $111.2 million in 1980 to $328.0 million in 1990. CRA redevelopment had spurred investment of more than $130.0 million in private and public monies. From 1980 to 1991, total public expenditures amounted to $54.9 million. [4]

In response to community demand for public safety, the CRA helped to fund the completion of a Chinatown Police Service Center. The $9.3-million Bamboo Plaza, a privately developed two-story pedestrian plaza and retail center, was also built with three levels of public parking above. Community facilities such as the Alpine Recreation Center, Kaiser Permanente Mental Health Center and the Chinatown Library were expanded, and street-side landscape on North Broadway and North Hill Street was also improved.

## 一九八零年代　　華埠重建計劃

一九八零年一月，經過兩年的社區討論，同時在社區的壓力下，洛市重建局終於通過華埠重建計劃，以提供社區迫切需要的住房，並使華埠繼續維持爲華人社區的文化和商業中心。一九八零年代，本區的其他重要重建目標包括開發經濟和鼓勵私人投資以創造就業機會，擴充育樂設施和增加文化活動。[1]

重建計劃包括六項低收入住宅計劃，加建育樂設施，改進商業區人文景觀。經由住屋輔助計劃使拉丁裔和非洲裔家庭遷入本區。今日拉丁裔、非洲裔和白人就如華人一般，是城裡許多餐館和商店的常客。

住房一直是華埠令人關切的議題之一，許多居民苦於工作技能不佳、教育程度有限、英語不流利，而自絕於美國社會之外，沉溺在貧窮、犯罪、族裔歧視和醫療保健短缺的痛苦中。

由於東南亞移民湧入，華埠傳統的經濟活動（如零售店、本地旅行社、餐館、車衣製造和銀行業）面臨重大的改變和挑戰。許多新移民具備雙語和文化能力，便參與國際貿易、以特定族裔的消費品爲主力商品的零售批發商，及各種服務業。資源和市場使華埠長久以來由華裔主導的經濟更爲多元化。[2]

一九八四年，半數的華埠商家爲越華所擁有，路邊的商招以三種語言呈現：中文、越文和英文。例如：在曉街和奧德街角的亞洲大樓有一座鐘樓即是仿西貢的鐘樓而建的，華埠九十餘年中草藥老店—永安堂，在正面的窗上展示用越文拼音的店名。[3]

在一九八零年代之前，華埠除了南邊外，已朝各方向發展：西向道奇球場、北往林肯崗、東朝工業區。大約二百一十萬平方呎已獲重建，絕大部分爲住宅區，地產價值成長三倍，由一九八零年的一億三千萬元上漲到一九九零年的三億二千八百萬元。重建局計劃帶動總計一億三千萬元政府和私人投資。從一九八零年到一九九一年，公共支出的總額達五千四百九十萬元。[4]

爲回應社區要求公共安全的呼聲，重建局撥款完成華埠警察服務中心。耗資九百三十萬元的安安商場是一棟二層樓設有行人步道和零售中心的私人開發案，上設三層樓公共停車場，沿北百老匯街和北曉街，還有庭園景觀設計。社區設施如愛盼娛樂中心、凱薩心理健康中心，以及華埠圖書館也同時擴建。

Michelle and Michael Wong with actor Keye Luke in the
stage play of "The Flower Drum Song" in 1985. Luke
began his film career in 1932. He also played the Number
One son in the first Charlie Chan film.

一九八五年，Michelle和Michael Wong與演員Keye Luke攝於
「花鼓歌」舞台前。Luke於一九三二年開始演員工作，曾在
陳查理的第一部電影中飾演陳查理之子。

Photo courtesy of Nancy Yee.

## ▶ Chinatown Cultural and Community Center

In January of 1988, with the support of Los Angeles council
members Gloria Molina and Michael Woo, the city appointed 25
Chinese-American community members to initiate the creation
of a multimillion-dollar Los Angeles Chinatown Cultural and
Community Center. The new Cultural Center's original plan
included an 800-seat theater, gymnasium, landscaped garden and
garage. The project currently is on hold and its future is unclear.

## 華埠文化和社區中心

一九八八年一月，在洛市市議員莫蓮娜和胡紹基的支持下，由洛
市任命二十五位社區人士，發起興建造價百萬元的洛市華埠社區
和文化中心。新文化中心的原始計劃包括一間八百個座位的戲院
、體育館、花園和停車場。這項開發案目前停滯不進，未來發展
不明。

A retail storefront in Chinatown, circa 1980s.

攝於一九八零年一家位於華埠的雜貨店前。

Photo courtesy of the Community
Redevelopment Agency of Los Angeles

## ▶ Chinese American Museum

The City of Los Angeles began planning for a Chinese American Museum (CAM). The museum will be the first in the Greater Los Angeles area dedicated to recording the stories of Chinese-American ancestors and pioneers. Its mission is to share the richness and vitality of the Chinese American experience that helped build the diverse community of Southern California today. With the support of the State of California, Friends of CAM and the Chinese Historical Society of Southern California (CHSSC), the 6,045-square-foot museum will be open by the year 2001 in the Garnier Building at the corner of Los Angeles Street and Arcadia Avenue, in the El Pueblo de Los Angeles Historical Monument.

Founded in 1975 and 1984 respectively, the CHSSC and the Friends of CAM are dedicated to promoting Chinese-American heritage and providing educational opportunities to the community through traveling photo exhibits, oral history workshops, Chinatown walking tours and field trips to Chinese American historical sites.

## 華人歷史博物館

此外，洛市也開始籌劃創辦一所華人歷史博物館，這將是大洛杉磯地區第一座用以紀念華裔先賢史蹟的博物館，博物館將生動展現華裔移民在塑造南加州為多元文化社區的豐富經歷。在華人歷史博物館之友會和南加州華人歷史學會的大力支持下，佔地六千零四十五平方呎的博物館預定在二千年零一年前，於洛杉磯街和亞凱迪亞街角的加尼爾大樓開放。

南加州華人歷史學會及華人歷史博物館之友會分別於一九七五年和一九八四年成立，主旨在發揚光大華人史蹟，並舉辦旅行攝影展、歷史講述座談、步行遊華埠和華人史蹟參觀等活動，提供社區學習的機會。

(From left to right:) Joseph Chen, Richard Wu, Li-Hwa Chan and C.T. Wu, former director of Chinese Daily News at the company's first office in Monterey Park..

（由左至右）鄭洵、吳彬銜、錢麗華和前世界日報主任吳炯造攝於蒙市報社門前

Photo courtesy of Chinese Daily News.

### ▶ The Emergence of the San Gabriel Valley Chinese Communities

Monterey Park continues to offer immigrants a prosperous suburban lifestyle, making it a popular destination for immigrant Chinese. It continues to be well known for its easy access to major freeways, affordable housing, good schools, diversity of people and some say superior "Feng Shui." [5]

Monterey Park and 12 neighboring cities in East and West San Gabriel -- Alhambra, Arcadia, El Monte, Pasadena, Rosemead, San Gabriel, San Marino, South Pasadena, Diamond Bar, Hacienda Heights, Rowland Heights and Walnut -- formed a clear Chinese concentration outside of Chinatown. Today, San Gabriel Valley has an estimated 200,000 ethnic Chinese, making the region one of the largest centers of Chinese immigrants in the U.S., according to the 1990 U.S. Census.

In the 1980s, housing prices skyrocketed in the San Gabriel Valley. Overseas Chinese were drawn to the Valley as a nice place to settle. Many used cash to buy houses, which at one point caused local banks to prohibit cash buying. [6]

The San Gabriel Valley population increased 359 percent from 1980 to 1990, and the number of Chinese businesses in the area grew signficantly from 604 in 1982 to 9,656 in 1996. According to the Immigration and Naturalization Service, Monterey Park was ranked the first choice of settlement for immigrants coming from Hong Kong, China and Taiwan. Two adjacent cities, Alhambra and Rosemead, ranked second and third respectively for Chinese newcomers.

### 聖蓋博谷的出現

蒙市繼續提供移民比較繁華的近郊生活條件，由於地近公路、房價合理、學區優秀、居民多元化，或是一般所說的風水佳，成為華裔移民熱衷的目的地。[5]

蒙市和東、西聖蓋博谷的十二個城市—阿罕布拉、亞凱迪亞、艾爾蒙地、帕莎迪納、柔似密、聖蓋博、聖瑪利諾、南帕莎迪納、鑽石吧、哈仙達崗、羅蘭崗和核桃市，在華埠之外形成華人聚居區。[6] 根據一九九零年人口普查，聖蓋博谷目前估計有二十萬華裔，是全美最大的華裔移民社區。

一九八零年代，聖谷房價飛漲，海外華人認為聖蓋博谷是定居的好區，許多人以現金買房子，一度使本地銀行禁止以現金購屋。[6]

從一九八零年到一九九零年，聖蓋博谷的人口增加百分之三百五十九，當地華人公司也由一九八二年的六百零四家增加到一九九六年的九千六百五十六家。根據移民局的統計，在來自香港、中國和台灣華裔移民的居住地選擇中，蒙市名列第一，鄰近的兩個城市—阿罕布拉和柔似密，則分別排名第二和第三。[6]

Lily Lee Chen, the first Chinese-American woman in the continental United States to be elected mayor, in 1984. Her efforts made Monterey Park an "All America City," fostering a spirit of citywide harmony and cooperation among the culturally diverse groups in the city.

一九八四年，陳李婉若成為美國本土第一位女性華裔市長。她努力在市內提倡族裔和諧合作，使蒙特利公園市獲得「全美模範城市的美譽」。

Photo courtesy of Lily Lee Chen

## ▶ Real Estate

The San Gabriel Valley Chinese community has an ethnic economic structure serving primarily Chinese Americans in the Valley. Real estate was the largest business in 1982. George Realty, a San Gabriel based realty company, averaged about $1 million a day in transactions for eight consecutive years. Home prices in San Marino averaged more than $540,000. The "Chineseness" of the place continued to draw Chinese immigrants to the community, especially those with limited English skills and job training. The other top five business categories were all services oriented, including medical doctors and dentists, restaurants, travel agencies, beauty salons and barbers.

### 房地產

聖蓋博谷華人社區是以服務華人為主的典型經濟結構。一九八二年，房地產是最熱門的生意之一，聖蓋博谷主要的地產公司—僑福地產連續八年平均每日的地產交易額大約都在一百萬元。聖瑪利諾的平均房價超過五十四萬元，但華裔社區對華裔新移民仍是一大吸引力，特別是對英語能力有限和本地工作經驗不足的新移民而言。其他五大行業均為服務業，包括醫生和牙醫、餐館、旅行社、美容院和理髮廳。

寂寞的辮子

Dr. Judy Chu was elected to the Monterey Park City Council, earning the largest share of votes in 1988. She campaigned under a platform of controlled-growth, ethnic diversity and racial harmony.

一九八八年，趙美心以最高票進入蒙市市議會。她的競選政見是控制發展，族裔多元和諧。

Photo courtesy of Judy Chu

# ▶ Global Economy

Chinese economic activities in the Los Angeles area contributed significantly to the global economy in the 1980s. Banking became a very important industry inside the San Gabriel Valley. There were over 40 Chinese-American financial institutions in Los Angeles in the late 1980s. East West Bank, Cathay Bank and General Bank were among the top ten largest commercial banks in terms of assets in Los Angeles County.  By the late 1980s, their combined assets would reach over $1.5 billion.   Other international trade businesses including import/export, air cargo service, custom houses and freight forwarding grew rapidly to 330 by 1996. This number accounted for over two-thirds of all Chinese businesses in Los Angeles County.  By the late 1980s, San Gabriel Valley was transformed from an ethnic cluster to a global business center.[7] In addition, the San Gabriel Valley Economic Partnership was planning to develop a Foreign Trade Zone (FTZ) to increase trade opportunities between the San Gabriel Valley and business communities in the Pacific Rim. Companies in the San Gabriel Valley can defer duty costs and preserve cash flow. Currently, the Pacific Place and the Pomona Complex are designated as the San Gabriel Valley Free Trade Zones.

To further enhance international relationships, the cities of Alhambra and Monterey Park established sister-city relationships with several cities in mainland China, Taiwan, Japan and Mexico.  They have acted as bridges between the East and West, vigorously promoting direct foreign investment and international trade. And the San Gabriel Valley has been playing a major role in promoting economic development and job opportunities.

Under the leadership of former Mayor Lily Chen and the efforts of the Chinese-American Committee of Monterey Park Chamber of Commerce, Monterey Park was named an "All America City" by the National Municipal League and USA Today in 1985. Citing effective citizenship and significant civic accomplishments brought through about a blending of private and public efforts, Monterey Park was one of eight national winners and the only California city honored that year. [8]

## 全球經濟

一九八零年代，洛杉磯地區的華人經濟活動對全球經濟貢獻良多，聖谷內的融資業成為重要行業之一，一九八零年代洛杉磯有四十多家華資金融機構，華美銀行、國泰銀行和萬通銀行在洛縣以其資產名列前十大商業銀行。到一九八零年代晚期，三家銀行的總資產超過十五億元。其他與全球經濟相關的行業包括進出口、空運服務、報關行和託運等，在一九九六年時，也快速成長到三百三十家，佔洛縣華商的三分之二以上。聖谷在一九八零年代末也轉型，由族裔聚集的社區化身為全球經濟前哨，在國際經濟活動中扮演重要角色。[7] 此外，聖谷經濟發展協會也於此時計劃開辦外貿區，以促進聖谷和亞太地區的商業和活動交流，位於聖谷的公司可享有延稅和現金周轉的便利，目前，聖谷的Pacific Place和Pomona Complex已規劃為外貿區。

為進一步延展國際關係，阿罕拉布拉市和蒙市分別與中國、台灣、日本和墨西哥等國的城市發展姊妹市關係，期望成為聯絡東西的橋樑，積極促進國外投資和國際業務交流。聖谷成為全球與地方經濟活動，以及創造工作機會的重要區域。

在前蒙市市長陳李婉若的領導，以及蒙市商會和華人委員會的共同努力之下，蒙市以政府與市民合作的傑出表現贏得一九八五年全國都市聯盟及今日美國評選為「全美模範城市」的榮譽。蒙市是當年獲此殊榮的全國八座城市之一，也是加州唯一上榜的城市。[8]

## ▶ Political Involvement

The growing Chinese community was still under-represented in municipal politics throughout the San Gabriel Valley. Only one city council member was Chinese American in the entire Valley in the 1980s. This phenomenon was contributed by the lack of strong democratic traditions in Asia and the lack of citizen status of the majority Chinese population. However, the variety of social backgrounds in the San Gabriel Valley also diversified its political orientations, views and actions. Generally speaking, the first-generation Chinese immigrants were more conservative with stronger cultural and political ties to their native countries. The second generation, or American-born Chinese, were more politically aware and better educated in leadership. Chinese Americans were more active politically than ever before, involving themselves in various sociopolitical movements and empowerment, joining civic and service groups, and serving on boards of education and volunteer committees.

One active Chinese-American civil rights advocacy group is the Organization of Chinese Americans (OCA) - - Greater Los Angeles Chapter. The OCA is a national non-profit, nonpartisan organization dedicated to securing the rights of Chinese American and Asian Pacific American citizens, and permanent residents through legislative and policy initiatives at all levels of government. In the late 1980s, the OCA was committed to public education, lobbying, and documentation of hate crimes. In recent years, it has been involved with organizing citizenship workshops, voter outreach and voter registration drives, and community educational forums.

In 1983 with broad community-based support, the Asian Pacific American Legal Center (APALC) was established to provide the growing Asian Pacific American community with multilingual legal services, providing education and civil rights advocacy in the areas of family law and domestic violence, consumer law, workers' rights, immigration, housing, civil rights, etc. Currently, Stewart Kwoh, president and executive director heads the center. Kwoh received a grant from the prestigious MacArthur Foundation for his civil rights work in the Asian-Pacific American community and his efforts in developing multiethnic partnerships.

In the early 1990s, an interethnic political coalition called the San Gabriel Valley Asian Pacific Americans for Fair Reapportionment, worked to increase minority representation at the state and federal levels. Many Chinese politicians and community leaders emerged and came to the Chinese communities for their support and advocacy. Below are some of the pioneering community and political leaders of Los Angeles Chinese community.

## 參政

聖谷一帶的市政圈裡，華人代表仍然不足。一九八零年代，聖谷整區只有一名華人市議員。這種現象可歸因於亞裔缺乏民主經驗，以及華人入籍人數有限。聖谷華人的社會背景、政治取向、觀點和作爲各不相同，大體而言，第一代華裔移民較保守，與祖國的文化和政治密切相連。第二代或是本地出生的華裔在政治方面所涉較深及廣，也曾接受較佳的領導統御訓練。華人參政比以往熱烈，並且加入市民和服務組織、教育委員和社區義工委員會。

美華會是大洛杉磯地區極爲活躍的華裔民權團體之一，傾力在各政府層級的立法和政策上，爲華裔公民和永久居民爭取平等權益。該會爲全國性、非營利、非政治性的組織。一九八六年，美華會更致力於社會、教育、遊說和仇恨犯罪追蹤等工作，近年來，更組織推廣公民入籍、選民登記和社區民權教育等計劃。

亞太美裔法律服務中心獲得廣大社區的支持，於一九八三年成立，是南加州居領導地位的社區團體之一，以多語言提供成長中的亞太裔社區，在家庭法、家庭暴力、消費者權益、勞工權利、移民、居住和民權等方面的服務，並宣導平權。目前，中心由郭志明擔任總裁和執行主任。由於他領導亞太裔社區爭取民權等的傑出表現，及在促進各族裔合作方面的努力，郭志明獲得知名的麥克阿瑟基金會的肯定與經費贊助。

一九九零年代早期，聖蓋博谷成立了一跨族裔的政治聯盟組織，主張平等任命，呼籲增加少數族裔在州和聯邦的代表席次。

許多華人開始活躍於政界和社區，他們來到華埠爭取華人的支持，並宣揚個人的政治理念。以下簡介活躍於洛杉磯華裔社區的社區人物和政界領袖。

### ▶ Daniel Wong

Dr. Daniel Wong was first elected to the Cerritos City Council in 1978. He served the city for 14 years, including two terms as mayor. During his 14-year tenure, he built closer relations between the United States and China, promoted economic development in the local community and improved health care in both countries. Wong was the first Chinese American to meet with Chinese Premier Li Peng after the Tiananmen Square crackdown in 1989. In 1996, congressional investigators accused Wong of accepting a campaign donation that allegedly was part of a Chinese government effort to influence American elections.[9] Wong was named as the "Talent of the Century" by Talent of the Century Magazine, printed in China in 1999.

### 黃錦波

黃錦波博士於一九七八年贏得喜瑞都市市議會選舉，是第一為當選市議員的華人，他服務喜市共十四年，期間並擔任兩次市長。任職市議會的十四年間，黃錦波致力拉近美中關係，促進地方社區經濟發展，協助改善兩國醫療保健措施。一九八九年天安門事件後，黃錦波是第一位會見中國總理李鵬的華裔美人。一九九六年，國會調查員控訴黃錦波接受中國欲影響美國選舉而贈予他的競選獻金。[9]一九九九年，中國印行的世紀天才雜誌封黃錦波為「世紀天才」。

The ground breaking ceremony for the Chinatown Branch Library, July 1981. Left to right: Dr. Ruby Louie, Mayor Tom Bradley, Dolores Wong.

一九八一年七月，華埠圖書館破土儀式，左至右，Dr. Ruby Louie, 市長布萊德雷和Dolores Wong。

Photo courtesy of the Friends of the Chinatown Library

Howard Jong (center) with Chief Pilot Lt. Bruce Logan (left) and Officer Paul Rasmussen (right). Jong, a pioneering Chinese-American aeronautical engineer spent three years in the 1980s improving and maintaining one of the nation's few light-weight surveillance airplanes used by the Monterey Park Police Department for patrol purposes. Today, the Ultralight is on display at the Smithsonian Institute in Washington, D.C.

Howard Jong（中）和警察局長Lt. Bruce Logan（左）和警官Paul Rasmussen（右），Jong是華裔航太工程師，一九八零年代，他花費三年時間改進和保養全國僅有的數架輕型偵察機，供蒙市警局做為巡邏之用。今日，超輕型飛機在華盛頓特區的Smithsonian博物館展出。

Photo courtesy of Howard Jong

寂寞的辮子

### ▶ David Lau

David Lau, current President of the Garvey School Board, was first appointed to the Board of Education of the Garvey School District in 1993. Since then, he has been an active board member. In 1998, he was elected president. Lau served as commissioner of the Monterey Park Community Relations Commission, president of the Monterey Park Recreation and Parks Commission and vice president of the Los Angeles County Human Relations Commission. In March 1999, Lau ran a political campaign for a seat in the Monterey Park City Council. He received 56.4 percent of the vote among Chinese Americans, the highest among seven candidates. However, he captured only 2,087 votes in all, losing by 31 votes to his opponent Fred Balderrama. Lau ranked first among five Asian candidates by the number of votes and ranked fourth among a total of 11 candidates. Lau is listed in the Who's Who Among Asian Americans in 1995, Who's Who in California in 1986 and received the Asian-American Achievement Award in 1985.

### 劉達強

嘉偉學區教育委員會現任主席。劉達強於一九九三年時獲派任為嘉偉學區教育委員後，即積極參與教委會事務，一九九八年，經教委會推選為主席。劉達強曾任蒙市社區關係委員會委員、蒙市公園和娛樂委員會主席、洛縣人際關係委員會副主席。一九九九年三月，劉達強參加蒙市議會選舉，獲得華人百分之五十六點四的選票，在落選的七名候選人中排名第一。他共得到二千零八十七張選票，僅差對手鮑德拉瑪（Fred Balderrama）三十一票，五位亞裔候選人中得票數最高，在十一為候選人中排名第四。劉達強曾列名一九九九年亞太裔名人錄、一九八六年加州名人錄，一九八五年獲亞美成就獎。

The Lee family at the Olympics banquet raised funds for China athletes in 1984. Back row, left to right: David Jr. and David Sr., a pioneer restaurant owner and community leader. Front row, left to right: Steven, Yukie and Sharon.

一九八四年，李家在奧運餐會上為中國選手募款。後排左至右：Daive Jr.、David Sr.，二人皆是餐館業主和社區領導人。前排左至右：Steven、Yukie和Sharon。

Photo courtesy of David and Yukie Lee

## ▶ Judy Chu

Dr. Judy Chu was elected to the Monterey Park City Council, earning the largest share of votes in 1988. She campaigned on a platform of controlled-growth, ethnic diversity and racial harmony. In 1992 and again 1994, Chu was elected as the Mayor of Monterey Park.

Chu initiated "Harmony Week" in October 1990. A citywide essay contest was held, prompting 450 children and adults to write about what it means to live in a multi-cultural society. Citizens, businesses and service clubs were recognized for promoting community harmony. Since then, Harmony Week in October has become a Monterey Park tradition.

## 趙美心

趙美心博士於一九八八年以最高票獲選進入蒙市議會。她以控制成長、社區族裔多元化和族裔和諧為競選政見主軸。一九九二年和一九九四年，趙美心兩度獲議會推選擔任市長。

趙美心於一九九零十月發起族裔和諧週，舉行全市作文比賽，吸引了四百五十名成人和孩子以「居住在多元文化的社會」為主題寫作，市府並且表彰對促進社區和諧有貢獻的市民、企業和服務性組織。和諧週自此成為蒙市每年十月的傳統活動。

## ▶ Julia Wu

Julia Wu, a member of the Los Angeles Community College District Board of Trustees, was first elected in 1987, and reelected in 1991 and 1995. She served as president of the board from 1991 to 1992. Governor Wilson appointed Trustee Wu to a six-year term on the California Community Colleges Board of Governors in 1992. She currently serves on the Los Angeles City Commission on the Status of Women and the Private Industry Council. Wu has received numerous honors and awards, including the 1990 Distinguished Service Award from the Monterey Park City Council and the 1995 Outstanding Local Elected Official Award from the White House Conference on Library and Information Services.

## 吳黎耀華

吳黎耀華是洛杉磯社區大學董事會董事，一九八七年首次獲選進入校董會，一九九一年和一九九五年兩度連任，一九九一年和一九九二年並擔任校董會主席。前加州州長威爾森於一九九二年任命吳黎耀華出任六年期的州長加州社區大學委員會委員，她目前是洛市婦女地位和私人企業協會委員。吳黎耀華獲頒的榮譽和獎項無數，包括一九九零年蒙市議會傑出服務獎，以及一九九五年白宮圖書館和資訊服務的傑出地方民選官員獎。

### ▶ Lily Lee Chen

In 1984, Lily Lee Chen was elected to be the first female Chinese-American mayor in the United States. She worked to stem the tide of anti-Chinese sentiment in Monterey Park. Chen encouraged Chinese business owners to put up multilingual signs voluntarily. She also cracked down on merchants who had erected signs without obtaining proper permits. Her efforts fostered a spirit of citywide harmony, acceptance and cooperation among the culturally diverse members of the community. Under her leadership Monterey Park was named an "All American City." Regional and national print media profiled Chen's career, gaining significant exposure for the successes of female Chinese Americans.

### 陳李婉若

一九八四年，陳李婉若獲選成為全美第一位女性華裔市長，在當時排華浪潮中陳李婉若鼓勵商家主動將商招改為多語言，拆下未取得許可而自行懸掛的商招。她努力培養全市的和諧氣氛，鼓勵市民在多元文化的社區中相互接受和合作。在她的領導之下，蒙市被評選為「全美模範城市」，地方和全國性報章雜誌均撰文介紹陳李婉若的生平，華裔婦女的成功表現備受稱道。

寂寞的辮子

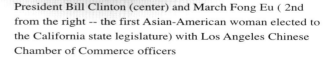

President Bill Clinton (center) and March Fong Eu ( 2nd from the right -- the first Asian-American woman elected to the California state legislature) with Los Angeles Chinese Chamber of Commerce officers

柯林頓總統（中）和余江月桂（右二，第一位加州民選女性官員）和羅省中華總商會的理事們。

Photo courtesy of Nancy Yee

### ▶ March Fong Eu

In 1966, March Fong Eu became the first Asian-American woman elected to the California state legislature. Her 20 years of service in the state assembly led her to become the first female Secretary of State in California after a record-setting three million votes in 1974. In 1994, while serving her fifth term, she was appointed as ambassador to Micronesia. Eu was named by the Ladies' Home Journal as one of America's 100 most important women in 1988.

### 余江月桂

一九六六年，余江月桂是第一位進入加州州議會的華裔女性。她在州議會二十年的資歷使她在一九七四年時，以三百萬的破紀錄高票獲選為加州州務卿。一九九四年，在她第五度擔任州務卿期間，獲派出使密克羅西亞。一九八八年，余江月桂獲Ladies Home Journal刊物選為全美最重要的一百名女性。

A mass rally for the Vincent Chin murder case in front of the Los Angeles City Hall on June 18, 1983. Concerned Chinese-American citizens urged the prevention of racial attacks, and to bring a federal prosecution for civil rights violations against the killers.

一九八三年六月十八日，大批華人在洛杉磯市府前集會抗議陳果仁被謀殺事件，呼籲維護華人權益、免於族裔攻擊迫害，要求聯邦以民法起訴並制裁兇手

Photo courtesy of Mary Yee.

Developed in 1984 by a community group with the support of the Community Redevelopment Agency, the Cathay Manor is a $23-million structure designed to house 270 senior citizens, a recreation center and a community service center.

興建於一九八四年，由社區人士倡議，在重建局的支持下，耗資二千三百萬元的國泰老人公寓峻工，可容納二百七十五位老人，附設娛樂中心和社區服務中心。

Photo courtesy of the Community
Redevelopment Agency of Los angeles

## ▶ Matthew Fong

Matthew Fong was elected as California Treasurer in 1995. During his four-year term he launched an aggressive campaign to make California the financial and commercial center of the Pacific Rim. In 1998, Fong ran for senator. He was defeated in the general election by his Democratic counterpart, Barbara Boxer, on November 2, 1998. Prior to his tenure as California Treasurer, he was vice chairman and a member of the State Board of Equalization from 1991 to 1994. He supported lowering taxes on manufacturing and reducing government regulations as a means to help businesses prosper in California.

### 鄺傑靈

一九九五年，鄺傑靈獲選爲加州財務長，在四年任期中，致力推動加州爲亞太地區的金融和商業中心。一九九八年，鄺傑靈角逐聯邦參議員，一九九八年十一月，不幸敗給民主黨對手芭芭拉.鮑克塞。在就任加州財務長之前的一九九一年至一九九四年間，他曾任加州銷售稅委員會委員，並曾任委員會副主席，他支持以降低廠商稅捐和減少政府條例限制的方式，協助加州企業成長。

## ▶ Michael Woo

Michael Woo gained recognition in 1985 as the first Asian American elected to the Los Angeles City Council. As a 41-year-old Democrat running for mayor of Los Angeles in 1993, he drew national attention. Woo, endorsed by President Clinton, was popular among young African-American and Asian-American voters. Woo condemned the police brutality in the widely publicized beating of Rodney King and called for racial harmony in the aftermath of the riots. Although he lost to Republican Richard Riordan, Woo inspired people of all races by focusing on the issues of justice and civil rights.

### 胡紹基

胡紹基於一九八五年獲選成爲進入洛市市議會的第一位華裔議員。一九九三年，時年四十一，胡紹基以民主黨人的身份競選洛市市長，引起全國矚目。胡紹基獲得當時美國總統柯林頓的支持，深受非裔和亞裔選民的歡迎，他抨擊警察在黑人羅尼‧金一案中使用暴力過當，並在洛市族裔衝突的暴亂後，極力呼籲種族和諧。雖然在選戰中失利，共和黨理查‧雷登當選洛市市長，胡紹基確實喚起各族裔起而正視並爭取民權和正義。

The Chinese United Methodist Church on 825 Hill Street. It was organized in Old Chinatown in 1887 and moved to its present location in 1947.

825曉街上的華人聯合美以美教會，一八八七年在舊中國城成立，一九四七年遷至現址。

Photo courtesy of the Community Redevelopment Agency of Los Angeles

## ▶ Sophie Wong

Sophie Wong was the first Asian American elected to serve on the Alhambra School Board in 1990. Wong was reelected to a third term in 1998. Currently, she is vice president of the board and president of Sophie C. Wong & Associates, a business development, real estate, marketing and public relations firm. Wong also became the first Asian/Chinese woman to serve as president of the Monterey Park Chamber of Commerce in 1988. She was a co-founder and past chairman of Golden Security Bank. Wong was named one of "Ten Important Power Brokers and Emerging Leaders in the San Gabriel Valley of Southern California" in the Los Angeles Business Journal in 1997, is listed as one of 500 notable women and named "Woman of the Year for 1998" by the American Biographical Institute, Inc.

## 黃趙企晨

一九九零年，黃趙企晨當選成爲第一位阿罕布拉學區的亞裔教育委員，一九九八年，她三度獲選，目前，她是教委會的副主席、黃趙企晨地產開發推廣和公關事務所總裁。一九八八年，她曾任蒙市商會第一位擔任會長的亞裔，也是第一位華裔女性會長。她也是金安銀行的創辦人之一，並曾任副董事長。一九九七年，黃趙企晨獲亞裔商業聯盟表揚爲「南加州聖蓋博地區具有影響力的地產經紀和領袖」，美國自傳協會也推選她爲一九九八年傑出女性，全美共有五百位女性獲得提名

The large painting of a fiery dragon on the building of today's United Commercial Bank was created by watercolor artist Tyrus Wong and restored in 1984 by Fu Deng Cheng.

聯合銀行牆上的兇猛威龍是水彩畫家Tyrus Wong的大作，一九八四年由Fu Deng Cheng修復。

Photo courtesy of the Community Redevelopment Agency of Los Angeles

## Wilbur Woo

Wilbur Woo has been known as the "godfather" and "unofficial mayor" of Chinatown for close to 40 years. He has been active in community organizations and service clubs that work to build a better community inside and outside Chinatown. He has served as national president of the Chinese American Citizens Alliance, president of the Los Angeles Chinese Chamber of Commerce, charter chairman of the Asian American National Business Alliance, founder and president of the California Taiwan Trade and Investment Council, overseas member of the Legislature of Taiwan National Assembly and as a member of the California State World Trade Commission. Currently, Woo is the Secretary of the Board of Cathay Bank, the oldest Chinese commercial bank in Los Angeles. Woo's strong sense of community service and involvement in the political arena have passed on to his son, Michael Woo, the first Asian-American city councilman in Los Angeles. Wilbur Woo was named as one of Los Angeles's top 20 "real powerful leaders" by Los Angeles Magazine in 1988.

## 胡國棟

四十多年來，胡國棟是華埠公認的「教父」和「民間市長」。他活躍於各社區和服務團體，致力於社區的繁榮發展。他曾任同源會全美會長、羅省中華總商會會長、亞美全國商業協會分會會長、加州台灣貿易投資協會創辦人和會長、中華民國僑選立委及加州世貿委員會委員。他目前是洛市最早成立的商業銀行－國泰銀行董事會書記。其子胡紹基承襲胡國棟對社區服務與參政的熱情，胡紹基是洛杉磯第一位華裔市議員。一九八八年，胡國棟獲洛杉磯時報雜誌推選為洛杉磯真正有影響力的前二十人之一。

The Pacific Alliance Medical Center on Hill and College is the former French Hospital -- the second oldest hospital in Southern California -- established in 1860 to serve what was once a large French community in the area

在曉街和大學街的協和醫療中心的前身是法國醫院，南加州第二悠久的醫院，一八六零年落成，為當時的法國社區服務。

Photo courtesy of the Community Redevelopment Agency of Los Angeles

寂寞的辮子

Michael Woo, the first Asian-American Los Angeles City Councilman and his father Wilbur Woo, the godfather and unofficial mayor of Chinatown. Wilbur Woo was named as one of the city's top 20 "real powerful leaders" by Los Angeles Magazine in 1988

洛市第一位華裔市議員胡紹基和其父胡國棟—華埠的民間市長和教父。一九八八年，洛杉磯時報雜誌推崇他爲二十位最有影響力的領導人之一

Photo courtesy of Wilbur Woo

## ▶ You Chung Hong

You Chung Hong was the first Chinese-American lawyer to be admitted to the bar in Southern California. From 1936 to 1952, Hong became an integral force in fighting the continuing congressional battles over immigration policy. For 50 years, Chinese-Americans regarded Y.C. Hong as the country's foremost Chinese attorney, a reputation based on his relentless work to repeal the Chinese Exclusion Act of 1882. At the age of 28, he was elected as president of the Los Angeles Chapter of the Chinese American Citizens Alliance (C.A.C.A.), which was founded in 1895 to insure the legal rights of its members and to secure equal economic and political opportunities for its members. He testified before the U.S. Senate Hearing Committee on immigration laws before he was 30 years old. [8]

## 洪耀宗

洪耀宗是全美和南加州第一位華裔律師，他一直在國會爲移民權益奮戰，五十多年來，由於他努力不懈，終於推翻了一八八二年的排華法案，華裔社區推崇他是全國最優秀的華裔律師。二十八歲時，他曾任同源會洛杉磯分會會長，同源會於一八九五年成立，主旨在保障會員們的合法權益，並爭取平等的政經發展機會。年未及三十，洪耀宗即曾在參議院移民法聽證會上作證。[8]

A Chinatown seamstress continues to work long hours at a minimum wage, as many did in the past.

華埠一家車衣廠還是一如過往，維持低工資、長時間的工作型態。

Photo courtesy of the Community Redevelopment Agency of Los Angeles

The 1990 census counted more than 60,000 residents living in Monterey Park, with Asians in the majority at 57.5 percent of the population, of which 63 percent were Chinese. In cities throughout the San Gabriel Valley, Asians showed impressive population growth since 1980: 289 percent growth in Alhambra, 371 percent in Rosemead, 732 percent in Walnut, 684 percent in Diamond Bar and 543 percent in Arcadia. Today, roughly one-third of San Marino's population is of Asian ancestry. The Chinese population in the San Gabriel Valley represented 49.21 percent of the total Chinese population in Los Angeles County in 1990. However, many ethnic Chinese are scattering around the Greater Los Angeles area without imbuing their cultural heritage.

一九九零年的人口普查顯示，超過六萬華人居住在蒙市，蒙市的亞裔佔全市人口的百分之五十七點五，而華人則佔其中的百分之六十三。自一九八零年起，聖蓋博谷各城市的亞裔人口更加顯著成長，其中阿罕布拉市增加百分之二百八十九，柔似蜜市增加百分之三百七十一，胡桃市增加百分之七百三十二，鑽石吧增加百分之六百八十四，亞凱迪亞增加百分之五百四十三。今日，聖瑪利諾市已有三分之一的亞裔居民。一九九零年時，聖蓋博谷的華裔人口佔洛杉磯縣華裔人口的百分之四十九點二一。而許多華裔雖散大洛杉磯其他地區，卻仍保持固有文化特色。

A recent Broadway street scene in Chinatown.

華埠百老匯街現代化的街景。

Photo courtesy of the Community
Redevelopment Agency of Los Angeles

# Chapter 10

*New Roles of Chinese Americans*
美裔美人的新角色定位

## The 1990s

The Chinese population reached 248,415 in 1990 according to the U.S. Bureau of Census, a 163.7 percent increase from 1980. This made the Chinese the largest and fastest growing ethnic group in Los Angeles County.

In the 1990s, more than 70 percent of the Chinese population in Los Angeles County is employed in white-collar professions. Nearly one of five homebuyers in Los Angeles County in 1992 had a Chinese surname.[1]

## 一九九零年代

根據全美人口普查，一九九零年華裔人口已達二十四萬八千四百一十五人，較一九八零年增加百分之一百六十三點七，華裔成為洛縣成長最快、人數最多的少數族裔。

一九九零年代，洛縣百分之七十以上的華裔為白領階級，一九九二年，有五分之一在洛縣置業者登記的姓名是華裔姓氏。[1]

寂寞的辮子

▶ **Dual-Society Chinatown**

A new wave of immigration over the last two decades created a dual society of entrepreneurs from Southeast Asia and the more assimilated, older merchants whose families emigrated from China many years ago. Ethnic Chinese from Southeast Asia have come to dominate businesses in Chinatown. Ginseng shops, jewelry stores, restaurants and swap-meet-style boutiques cater to other ethnic newcomers.

Chinatown is now a multi-ethnic community struggling to compete with businesses in the San Gabriel Valley. Less profitable businesses have demanded rent reductions throughout Chinatown. According to David Louie, a fourth generation Chinese American and a commercial real estate agent, more than 20 retail and office buildings in Chinatown went into foreclosure in 1995, representing one-fourth of Chinatown's business district. [2]

To help turn blighted real estate into viable sites for business, the Mayor's economic team proposed to transform the 50-acre "Cornfield" next to Chinatown into an industrial park in 1999 which is predicted to bring 1,000 jobs. The Cornfield is an abandoned railroad freight yard located east of Chinatown between North Broadway and North Spring Street. Companies involved in manufacturing, food processing, importing and exporting are targeted as potential tenants for the development. [3]

The Cornfield proposal has brought growing controversy from a newly formed coalition of the environmentalists and Chinatown activists called the Chinatown Yard Alliance. The group's vision is to create green space, schools, affordable housing and mixed uses that Chinatown residents need, based upon the longtime Central City North Community Plan. Three major eastside political leaders have joined forces to call for an Environmental Impact Report to evaluate alternative uses.

In August of 2000, the Los Angeles City Council approved the Majestic Realty's proposal to turn the Cornfield into a 900,000 square foot light manufacturing and industrial park. With the city's help, Majestic Realty has received $14 million in federal funding for job creation and site cleanup.

In 1999, the Chinese Chamber of Commerce of Los Angeles and the newly formed Los Angeles Chinatown Business Council worked to establish a property-based Business Improvement District (BID). The BID's objective is to facilitate the rebirth of historic Chinatown as a culturally-defined, economically vibrant and socially engaging community. Programs include sidewalk cleanup, graffiti eradication and private security patrols.

## 新舊融合的華埠

近二十年的東南亞新移民潮創造了新興企業家與七十年前來自中國的老商號融合的華埠。來自東南亞的華人主導華埠經濟，經營華埠近百分之九十的生意，蔘行、珠寶行、餐館和禮品店為思鄉情切的新移民服務。

華埠現已儼然是一多元族裔社區，汲汲於爭取漸湧向聖蓋博谷的華裔居民和商業活動。華埠生意差的業者要求減租，當業主無法付出貸款時，物業即遭到銀行收回拍賣。第四代華裔移民，也是商業物業經紀David Louie表示，一九九五年，華埠有超過二十家的零售店和辦公樓被銀行收回拍賣，佔華埠商業區的四分之一。[2]

為了扭轉地產頹勢，一九九九年，洛杉磯市市長提出一項開發案，將緊臨華埠的五十畝玉米田改建為工業園區，估計可創造一千個就業機會。玉米田位於華埠東區，在北百老匯和北士丙令街之間，是一廢棄鐵路貨運站的舊址。開發區擬吸引工廠、食品加工業，和進出口業公司。[3]

此項玉米田開發案引起社區廣泛爭議，環保人士和華埠社區活躍人士組成聯盟，根據原有的城中北區開發計劃，希望以華埠居民的需求為主，開闢綠地、興建學校和住宅。三位東區主要的政界領導人士加入聯盟，要求就替代方案進行環境影響評估。

二千年八月，洛市議會通過Majestic地產公司將玉米田改為佔地九十萬平方呎的輕工業和製造業園區。在市府的協助下，Majestic地產公司已獲得一千四百萬元聯邦經費，做為開創工作機會和工程整地之用。

一九九九年，羅省中華總商會和新近成立的城中商會合作進行商業改進區計劃，擬議重建華埠成為文化、經濟和社會並重的社區中心，相關計劃包括人行道清潔、清理塗鴉和安全巡邏等。

David Lau ran for re-election to the Garvey School District Board of Education in November 1997 with a slogan of "Let's Leap Together with Our Children into the 21st Century." In 1998, he was elected as president of the Garvey School Board.

一九九七年十一月，劉達強高唱「帶領孩子們走向二十一世紀」，競選嘉偉學區教委連任，一九九八年，他當選嘉偉學區教委會主席。

Photo courtesy of David Lau

Sophie Wong was the first Asian American elected to serve on the Alhambra School Board in 1990. She was listed as one of the 500 notable women in the U.S. by the American Biographical Institute, Inc. in 1998.

一九九零年，黃趙企晨是第一位當選阿罕布拉學區教委的華裔人士。一九九八年，她獲全美傳記學會列名為全美五百位知名女性。

Photo courtesy of Sophie Wong

### ▶ Chinese-American Investment

Chinese immigration has brought capital, human resources and international trade to Los Angeles. The infusion of Chinese investment has been an important factor in the county's economic recovery. According to the U.S. Department of Commerce, the combined two-way trade between Los Angeles and China, Hong Kong and Taiwan reached $41.5 billion with most financing by Asian banks in 1996. [4] Also, in January 1998, Cathay Bank, East West Bank, United National Bank, Standard Savings Bank and Trust Bank united to form the San Gabriel Valley Development Corporation with the mission to provide financial assistance to small businesses in San Gabriel Valley that may have difficulty in obtaining financing through traditional lending channels. Some predicted that Taiwanese banks will invest billions of dollars in the Los Angeles area over the next five years and thus could do more local business and eventually become major players in the local consumer and business banking markets.

As Southern California's economy continues to rebound, the recent immigrants from Taiwan, Hong Kong, China and Southeast Asia, have proven to be the region's most aggressive economic players. In 1997, Chinese investors and entrepreneurs were buying large properties at prices about 50 percent of previous purchase prices. Among these properties were several downtown Los Angeles office towers and hotels, including the Biltmore, the Bonaventure, the Beverly Wilshire, the Intercontinental and the Hiltons at Universal City and LAX. The Taiwanese have also been known for their hotel/motel investments. [5] An informal survey indicated that about one-third of motels in Southern California are owned by Chinese. Of loans from Chinese-American banks, 59 percent were real estate related, compared to 38 percent in other California banks. [6]

In addition to office buildings and hotels, Chinese capitalists can be found in companies ranging from restaurants and computer makers in the San Gabriel Valley to textile, garment and other "soft goods" industries in Orange County. The retail strip along Valley Boulevard through Alhambra into the heart of the San Gabriel Valley has been successful. The largest retail complex is San Gabriel Square in the City of San Gabriel. It occupies a land area of 560,000 square feet with 220,000 leasable square feet and 1040 parking spaces. It includes 100 stores, anchored by a Chinese Tawa Supermarket with a floor area of 45,000 square feet and a department store occupying an area of 52,500 square feet.

In 1994, nine Chinese-American companies were noted in "Hoover's Guide Among The Top 500 Largest Companies in Southern California" based on sales revenues. They were: Kingston Technology Company; Bugle Boy Industries Inc.; ViewSonic Corporation; Advanced Logic Research, Inc.; Tetra Tech, Inc.; Panda Management Company, Inc.; Watson Pharmaceuticals, Inc.; GBC Bancorp and Cathay Bancorp, Inc. [7]

The Summer Reading Club at the Chinatown Branch Library, 1998.

一九九八年，華埠圖書館的暑期讀書會。

Photo courtesy of the Chinatown Branch Library

## 華人投資

華裔移民為洛杉磯帶來資金、人才和企業家，華人資金成為洛縣經濟復甦的要素。一九九六年美國商業部的一項統計顯示，洛杉磯與中、港、台三地的雙向貿易達四百一十五億元，且融資機構多為亞裔銀行。洛杉磯商業週刊報導指出，一九九三年起，華人在銀行和地產方面的投資已逾十億元。[4] 一九九八年一月，國泰銀行、華美銀行、匯通銀行、中興儲蓄銀行和聯華銀行聯合成立聖蓋博谷開發公司，專為聖蓋博谷小型商業提供融資協助，紓解經由傳統借貸管道融資所遭遇的困境。傳言在未來的五年內，來自台灣的金融機構將在洛杉磯挹注數十億元資金，準備積極投入地方經濟，在消費者和商業銀行的市場上大顯身手。

南加州經濟持續反彈，來自台灣、香港、中國大陸和東南亞的新移民帶來的活力已證實他們是本區經濟圈積極活動的重要角色。一九九七年，華裔投資人和創業家以低於先前交易價的百分之五十購得地產，多筆交易中有不少是在城中的大樓和酒店，包括巴爾地摩、朋納凡丘、比佛利山威爾樹、城中大陸、影城希爾頓和洛杉磯機場希爾頓，台灣人因他們在酒店和旅館的投資而聲名大噪。[5] 一項非正式的調查指出，南加州大約有三分之一的汽車旅館為華人所有，相對於加州其他銀行的百分之三十八，華資銀行的融資業務有百分之五十九與地產相關。[6]

除了辦公大樓和酒店，華人在聖蓋博谷投資的餐館、電腦公司，以及橙縣的紡織和車業衣也很普遍。阿罕布拉市山谷大道上的零售地帶延長進入聖蓋博谷中心，生意鼎盛，在聖蓋博市的聖蓋博廣場更是該區最大的零售商場，佔地五十六萬平方呎，其中二十二萬平方呎可租用，另有一千零四十個停車位，商場裡有一百家商店，其中一家四萬五千平方呎的台式超市，以及五萬二千五百平方呎的百貨公司為主要商號。

一九九四年，有九家華裔公司以其年度業績，登上胡佛指引的南加州前五百大公司。這九家公司是：Kingston Technology Company、號角男孩、ViewSonic Corporation、Advanced Logic Research, Inc.、Tetra Tech, Inc., Panda Management Company, Inc., 華生製藥廠、萬通集團、國泰集團。

Actress Beulah Quo reads to children at the Chinatown Library during National Library Week, 1996.

一九九六年，演員郭鄧如喬在全國圖書館週時，在華埠圖書館為孩子們說故事。

Photo courtesy of the Chinatown Branch Library

寂寞的辮子

### ▶ Kingston Technology Company

Kingston was founded in 1987 by Shanghai-born John Tu and Taiwan-born David Sun. Kingston is the world's second biggest maker of add-on memory modules for personal computers. It developed an edge over its competitors by establishing close relationships with its 3,000 suppliers and distributors. Kingston has been named as one of the "100 Best Companies to Work for in the U.S." for the past two consecutive years by Fortune Magazine. The advancements in software and growing use of the Internet have increased the demand for memory upgrades. Kingston also designs and manufactures customized processor, networking and storage upgrade products. In 1994, Kingston revealed that its 300 workers each accounted for about $2.7 million in sales. Kingston reported $1 billion in sales revenues in 1997.

### Kingston Technology Company

Kingston由出生於上海的杜紀川和來自台灣的孫大衛於一九八七年攜手創辦，是全球生產個人電腦記憶晶片的第二大廠商，該司公和三千家供應商和經銷商建立起密切關係，以此獨樹一幟，使競爭廠商瞠乎其後。Kingston連續兩年獲財星雜誌提名爲全美前一百大最佳僱主。軟體升級和網際網路風行使增加記憶體的需求量也隨之起飛。Kingston也設計生產特別處理器，以及網路和增加儲存量的產品，一九九四年，Kingston對外表示，該公司的三百名員工每人平均創造了兩百七十萬的銷售業績，至一九九七年，Kingston年度業績已達十億元。

### ▶ ViewSonic Corporation

ViewSonic was founded in 1990 by James Chu, an immigrant from Taiwan. Chu started out selling keyboards, first in Taiwan and then in California, beginning in 1986. In 1990, he spotted a market niche for a company that could produce high-end monitors for lower prices than those being offered by the established top brands. ViewSonic has established itself as a leading worldwide provider of high-performance color computer monitors and uninterruptible power supplies (UPS). Today, ViewSonic competes successfully with international giants such as Sony, Mitsubishi and Philips. It has become a household name in the monitor business. In January of 1998, the company received the Product of the Year Award for 21" Monitors from PC Magazine. In 1997, ViewSonic was noted by the Los Angeles Business Journal as one of the fastest growing private companies in Los Angeles County. It reported $941 million in revenues in 1998, employing close to 700 people with five offices

### ViewSonic Corporation

ViewSonic是台灣移民朱家良於一九九零年創辦。朱家良於一九八六年起，先後在台灣和加州銷售鍵盤，一九九零年，他認定市場需要一生產低價位的高級電腦顯像器的公司，而非售價昂貴的名牌產品的利基。ViewSonic現已發展成爲全球生產彩色電腦顯像器和無限供電系統的知名領導廠商，ViewSonic現與新力、三菱和菲利普等國際巨人比肩競爭而毫不遜色，成爲眾所周知的顯像器品牌。一九九八年一月，ViewSonic的二十一吋顯像器獲PC Magazine的年度產品大獎。一九九七年，ViewSonic獲得洛杉磯商業週刊評選爲洛縣成長最快速的私人公司之一。一九九八年，公司年收入已達九億四千一百萬元，五間分公司共有員工近七百人。

## ▶ Watson Pharmaceuticals, Inc.

Watson Pharmaceuticals, Inc. was founded by Allen Chao in 1984 with $4 million in start-up capital from family members. Watson introduced its first drug, Furosemide, in 1985. Since then it has added about 60 drugs to its product line. Watson grew in the highly competitive generic drug market by avoiding highly competitive high-volume drugs and focusing on difficult-to-copy drugs such as Ansendin and Loxapine. Watson went public in 1993. In 1995, the company bought its rival, Circa Pharmaceuticals, in a near $600 million stock swap, giving Watson access to two exclusive drugs. In 1998, Watson reported sales revenues of $556 million. WPI was rated by Smart Money magazine as one of the best performing stocks in 1997.

## 華生製藥廠

趙宇天於一九八四年以向家人借來的四百萬元資金起家，成立華生製藥廠，一九八五年生產第一項藥品Furosemide，自此之後，又有近六十種藥品投入生產線。在藥品市場上，華生避開競爭激烈的大量生產藥品，將生產集中於同質藥品，以及較難複製的藥品，如 Ansendin和Loxapine。一九九三年，華生製藥廠上市，一九九五年，以價值六億元的股票交換，買下對手斯爾卡藥廠，華生因此取得兩種獨家生產藥品。一九九八年，華生的年銷售已達五億五千六百萬元。華生製藥廠股票一九九七年獲Smart Money雜誌評選為最佳股票之一。

### ▶ Bugle Boy Industries Inc.

Bugle Boy was founded by Dr. William Mow in 1977. Bugle Boy is one of the largest privately held apparel companies in the country, selling its products in more than 7,000 department stores as well as its own retail factory outlet stores. Bugle Boy makes casual clothing and accessories primarily for men and boys. Recently its product line has expanded to include jeans, shorts and accessories such as caps, watches, and sunglasses for women and girls. Bugle Boy has become a brand well-known for its design, quality and low price. In 1998, Bugle Boy reported an annual sales of $529 million.

### 號角男孩司公司

一九七七年毛昭寰創辦號角男孩，成為洛縣最大的私人成衣公司，產品在七千多家百貨公司和廠商直營店銷售。號角男孩的產品以男士和男孩的休閒服飾為主，生產線現已擴及仕女和年輕女孩的牛仔褲、短褲，以及帽子、手錶、太陽眼鏡等配件。號角男孩的品牌以設計、品質和低價位聞名。一九九八年的銷售額達五億二千九百萬元。

The swap-meet style, open-air shopping mini-mall on North Broadway. Ninety percent of its businesses are operated by ethnic Chinese from Southeast Asia.

北百老匯街上的露天市集，百分之九十九的生意人都是來自東南亞的華裔。

Photo courtesy of the Community Redevelopment Agency of Los Angeles

Street scene on modern-day Hill Street looking north.

曉街朝北看的現代街景。

Photo courtesy of the Community Redevelopment Agency of Los Angeles

New Chinatown continues to serve as an important social center for the elderly.

新中國城仍是老人家們的社交中心。

Photo courtesy of the Community Redevelopment Agency of Los Angeles

寂寞的辮子

### ▶ Tetra Tech, Inc.

Tetra Tech was founded in 1966 by four scientists as a coastal and marine engineering firm, specializing in environmental issues, underwater optics and marine robotics. Li-San Hwang joined the firm in 1967 as Chairman and President. The company went public in 1991. The company operates in three areas: resource management, telecommunications and infrastructure. Demand for Tetra Tech's services is driven primarily by federal, state and local laws and regulations relating to water resources and the environment. Acquisitions in 1994 and 1995 included Simons, Li & Associates, Hydro-Search, PRC Environmental Management and KCM. Tetra Tech, Inc. reported $382 million in sales with more than 3,600 employees in 1998.

### Tetra Tech, Inc.

一九六六年，四位科學家創辦 Tetra Tech, Inc.海洋工程公司，專精於環境、海底光纖和海底自動機械。黃立三在一九六七年加入公司，擔任董事長兼總裁，公司於一九九一年上市。資源管理、通訊傳播和基礎工程是公司的三大業務，客戶多爲符合聯邦、州及地方政府的水資源和環境法規而來。一九九四年和一九九五年間收購的公司有李棟材事務所、Hydro-Search、PRC環境管理公司和KCM。Tetra Tech, Inc.一九九八年業績達三億八千七百萬元，共有員工三千六百多人。

### ▶ Panda Management Company, Inc.

Founded in 1973 by Andrew Cherng, Panda Management Company (PMC) is one of the nation's largest quick-service Chinese food chains. With a winning formula tailored to suburban palates and his father's expertise as a well-known chef in mainland China, the Cherngs began expanding their business at a lightning pace in 1983. Now, Cherng has a chain of more than 254 Panda Express fast-food outlets, 13 Panda Inn and Panda Chinese restaurants and 7 Hibachi-San Japanese restaurants. PMC operates in 34 states and Japan. In 1998, PMC reported $194 million in sales with more than 3,600 employees nationwide.

### Panda Management Company, Inc.

程正昌於一九七三年創辦Panda Management Company，現爲全國最大的中式快餐連鎖店。特殊的口味，以及原中國大陸名廚程父的秘方，程氏家族於一九八三年開始以閃電般的速度擴大經營。現在，程家共有超過二百五十四家快餐連鎖店、十三家餐館，和七家日式料理店。PMC餐點風行全美三十四州和海外的日本。一九九八，PMC年銷售額共一億九千四百萬元，全國共有三千六百多名員工。

The Los Angeles Public Library Chinatown Branch at Castelar Elementary School.

洛杉磯圖書館設在嘉士德樂小學內的華埠分館。

Photo courtesy of Bill Chun Hoon.

▶ **Cathay Bancorp, Inc.**

Cathay Bancorp, Inc. is the holding company for Cathay Bank. Founded in 1962 by a group of community business leaders, Cathay Bank became the first Chinese-American community bank in Southern California dedicated to providing a full line of commercial banking services to its community in Los Angeles. It started with modest capital of $550,000 and a staff of seven operating in a 1,000-square-foot storefront office on Broadway in Chinatown.

In 1994, Cathay Bank received the "10-year Continued Premier Performing Bank Award" by the Findley Reports, placing it among the top six ranking California financial institutions for safety, strength and performance. With its strong financial strength and solid organizational structure, today Cathay Bank is ranked as the fifth largest commercial bank in Los Angeles County with assets over $2 billion. Today it operates 18 offices in Southern California, two offices in New York, one loan production office in Houston and two overseas offices in Hong Kong and Taiwan. Cathay Bancorp reported annual sales revenues of $131 million with more than 500 employees in 1998.

## 國泰集團

國泰集團為國泰銀行的控股公司。國泰銀行於一九六二年,由多位社區領袖聯合創辦,是南加州第一家華資社區銀行,提供洛縣社區完整的商業銀行服務。創辦資本僅五十五萬元,七名員工在華埠百老匯街一千呎大的分行開始營業。

一九九四年,國泰銀行獲Findley Report的連續十年績優銀行獎,躋身加州最安全、實力最強、表現最好的前六大銀行。國泰銀行以其雄厚的財力和健全的組織,現排名洛縣第五大商業銀行,總資產二十億元,全加州共有十八間分行,紐約有二間分行,另在休斯頓設有貸款中心,在台、港並有辦事處。國泰集團一九九八年總收入達一億三千一百萬元,員工共有五百多人。

### ▶ GBC Bancorp

GBC Bancorp is the bank holding company for General Bank. In order to serve the Chinese community, Taiwanese immigrants founded General Bank in 1980 with initial capital of $6.6 million.  Over the years, the bank has established itself as a premier provider of trade finance and international banking services to the Chinese community.  Its primary strength is linking California with Pacific Rim countries, with particular concentration on international trade financing for small- to medium-sized companies. In 1997, General Bank was named as one of the top ten outstanding participating financial institutions by the California Export Finance Office (CEFO).  Today, General Bank operates 16 branches in California with assets of $1.5 billion. In 1998, the company reported annual revenues of $133 million with 330 employees.

### 萬通集團

萬通集團是萬通銀行的控股公司。為了服務華裔社區，台灣移民在一九八零年創辦萬通銀行，創業資本共六百六十萬元。多年來，萬通銀行已發展成為華裔社區的主要銀行，提供國際貿易服務，專精於聯繫加州與太平洋沿岸國家之間中小型企業的國貿活動之一。一九九七年，萬通銀行獲加州出口融資處評為前十大傑出融資機構。萬通銀行在加州現有十六間分行，總資產十五億元，一九九八年之年收入為一億三千三百萬元，共有員工三百三十人。

Over 80 percent of Castelar Elementary School's students are Chinese.

嘉士德樂小學有百分之八十以上的學生為華裔。

Photo courtesy of the Community Redevelopment Agency of Los Angeles

Castelar Elementary School on Yale Street is the second oldest operating elementary school in the Los Angeles Unified School District. It is the first school in the district with trilingual instruction (Chinese, English, Spanish).

耶魯街上的嘉士德樂小學是洛杉磯學區歷史第二悠久的，並繼續授課的學校，也是學區第一所以三種語言（中、英、西）教學的學校。

Photo courtesy of the Community Redevelopment Agency of Los Angeles

## ▶ Advanced Logic Research

Advanced Logic Research (ALR) was founded by engineer/entrepreneur Gene Lu in 1984. ALR is a pioneer in open, multi-processor, Intel-based PC servers. Based in Irvine, ALR introduced the first 386 computer and has frequently upstaged its larger competitors with innovative systems and unique solutions. The Pentium chip-based server is one of the award-winning ALR Revolution families. Today, ALR is the subsidiary of Gateway, Inc. which is the number two direct marketer of PC's in the U.S., behind global leader Dell. In 1998, Gateway reported $7.5 billion in sales revenues.

## Advanced Logic Research

Advanced Logic Research（ALR）於一九八四年由工程師Gene Lu創辦。總部設於爾灣的ALR是開放式、多晶片、英代爾型的個人電腦伺服器先驅，首先推出第一台386電腦之後，又經常以創新的系統與獨特的系統處理令大公司刮目相看。Pentium 晶片的伺服器是ALR家族的得獎產品之一。ALR現爲僅次於Dell的全美個人電腦直銷第二大公司Gateway, Inc.的分支機構。一九九八年，Gateway的年銷售額達七十五億元。

In 1996, according to Chinese System Media, Inc., the restaurant business was ranked as the second largest Chinese business in Los Angeles County. Of the 880 Chinese restaurants in Los Angeles County that year, 503 were in the San Gabriel Valley cities. Panda Express Restaurant, Sam Woo Restaurant and 99 Ranch Market were among the successful businesses. Two years later, in 1998, ten Chinese-American companies were noted by the Los Angeles Business Journal as among the leading companies in Los Angeles County.

一九九六年，根據華商年鑑，餐館業是洛縣華商從事的第二大行業。當年洛縣的有八百八十間餐館，其中五百零三家在聖蓋博谷城市，Panda Express 餐館、三和皇宮和九九超市是其中的佼佼者。兩年後，於一九九八年，有十家華商獲洛杉磯商業週刊評選為洛縣領先企業。

Johnny Yee presented a plaque to Bruce M. Powell, Superintendent, inscribed with the following words: "In appreciation to the staff of the Golden Spike National Historic Site for recognizing the contributions made by Chinese railroad workers."

Johnny Yee將一面獎牌贈予總監 Bruce M. Powell，上面寫著「感謝金釘全國歷史會肯定華裔鐵路工人的貢獻」。

Photo courtesy of Chinese Historical Society of Southern California

On May 10, 1998, the Chinese were honored at the 47th Anniversary of the Golden Spike event at the Golden Spike National Historic Site in Promontory Summit for their contributions in helping to build the Central Pacific Railroad. With help from his brother John, Johnson Yee drives a spike at the site where the transcontinental railroad was completed 130 years ago in Promontory. Johnson Yee hammers the gold from his great-grandfather's tooth cap onto the spike to commemorate Chinese laborers who worked on the railroad. Left to right: Franklin Mah, Johnson Yee, Gardner Barlow and Johnny Yee in front of the Central Pacific's locomotive Jupiter.

一九九八年五月十日，金釘歷史會舉行第四十七屆金釘紀念會，表彰華人對修築中央太平洋鐵路的貢獻。Johnson Yee在弟弟John的協助下，把祖父的金牙套打入在一百三十年前完工的跨陸鐵路的一支釘子上。以紀念修築鐵路的華工。左至右，Franklin Mah, Johnson Yee, Gardner Barlow 和Johnny Yee在Central Pacific's Locomotive Jupiter。

Photo courtesy of Johnny Yee.

Approximately 600 children attended the Chinese Confucious Temple Chinese School after regular school hours and on weekends. In this kindergarten class, students are learning how to read and write in Chinese. Here, teacher Guan Shao Ping teaches vocabulary.

大約有六百個孩童在正規學校課後和週末，到中華孔廟學校上課。幼稚園班上學生學習中文讀寫。關曉萍（譯音）老師教導辭彙。

Photo courtesy of Michael Smith

From left to right: Celena and Crystal Smith (the author's 5-year and 7-year old daughters) and Melissa Wong showed their ethusiasm where they study at the Chinese Confucius Temple of Los Angeles in April 2000.

由左至右：史慧玲、史慧晶（作者之女，時年五歲、七歲）與Melissa Wong於二千年四月在洛杉磯中華孔廟學校認眞學習中文。

Photo courtesy of Icy Smith

# Prominent Chinese-American Companies in Los Angeles County　洛杉磯主要華商企業

| No.<br>公司 | Company<br>公司 | Designation<br>特點 | Rank<br>排名 | Revenues<br>'97 (in mil)<br>年收入 | 5-yr<br>Average<br>Return on<br>equity<br>五年平均<br>淨值回收 | % Growth<br>in revenues<br>from1995 -97<br>業績成長 | Company<br>Description<br>公司簡介 | City<br>所在城市 |
|---|---|---|---|---|---|---|---|---|
| 1. | Avus Systems and Peripherals Inc. | Fastest Growing Private Co.<br>成長最快的<br>私人公司 | 14 | $55 | n/a | 214% | manufacturer and distributor of PC hardware and peripherals<br>生產經銷電腦組件 | City of Industry<br>工業市 |
| 2. | Cathay Bancorp<br>國泰集團 | L.A.'s Most Profitable Public Company<br>獲利最高的公司<br>Largest Minority-Owned Business<br>規模最大的<br>少數族裔企業 | 52<br><br>7 | $112 | 12.31 | n/a | commercial bank<br>商業銀行 | Los Angeles<br>洛杉磯 |
| 3. | G.B.C. Bancorp<br>萬通集團 | L.A.'s Most Profitable Public Company<br>獲利最高的公司<br>Largest Minority-Owned Business<br>規模最大的<br>少數族裔企業 | 44<br><br>8 | $111 | 13.85 | n/a | commercial bank<br>商業銀行 | Los Angeles<br>洛杉磯 |
| 4. | Maxtech Holding Inc. | Fastest Growing Private Co.<br>成長最快的<br>私人公司 | 77 | $142.10 | n/a | 46% | distributor of computer peripherals<br>經銷電腦組件 | Cerritos<br>喜瑞都 |
| 5. | Mitsuba Corp. | Largest Private Company<br>規模最大<br>私人公司<br>Fastest Growing Private Co.<br>成長最快的<br>私人公司 | 66<br><br>56 | $175 | n/a | 72% | wholesale computer manufacturer<br>電腦製造批發 | La Verne<br>拉汶 |
| 6. | Ocean Duke Corp. | Fastest Growing Private Co.<br>成長最快的<br>私人公司 | 84 | $112 | n/a | 42% | seafood importer and distributor<br>海產進口經銷 | Torrance<br>托侖斯 |
| 7. | Panda Management Co., Inc. | Largest Private Company<br>規模最大<br>私人公司<br>Fastest Growing Private Co.<br>成長最快的<br>私人公司 | 96<br><br>69 | $169 | n/a | 34% | Chinese quick service and full-service restaurants<br>中式快餐和餐館 | South Pasadena<br>南帕莎迪納 |
| 8. | Premio Computers | Largest Private Company<br>規模最大<br>私人公司<br>Fastest Growing Private Co.<br>成長最快的<br>私人公司 | 78<br><br>85 | $150 | n/a | 41% | computer desktop and server manufacturer<br>製造電腦系統<br>和伺服器 | City of Industry<br>工業市 |
| 9. | Tetra Technology | Largest Public Company<br>規模最大公司<br>L.A.'s Most Profitable Co.<br>獲利最高的公司 | 76<br><br>24 | $247 | 18.57 | n/a | environmental consulting and engineering services<br>環境工程顧問公司 | Pasadena<br>帕莎迪納 |
| 10. | ViewSonic Corporation | Largest Private Company<br>規模最大<br>私人公司<br>Fastest Growing Private Co.<br>成長最快的<br>私人公司 | 11<br><br>27 | $826 | n/a | 27% | high-tech computer display technology<br>高科技電腦顯示器 | Walnut<br>核桃市 |

Source: Los Angeles Business Journal Book of List, 1999
來源：1999洛杉磯商業周刊

寂寞的辮子

174

▶ In addition to the above new generation of Chinese business leaders, Chinese have also been the leading force behind the expansion of the wholesales toy business in downtown Los Angeles.

**Toy Manufacturing Industry   Mega Toy**

Charles Woo, the would-be Ph.D. physicist, and Peter Woo, a former Hong Kong stockbroker, created the billion-dollar Toytown industry in downtown Los Angeles, enhancing Los Angeles' position as the nation's hub for transpacific trade in the 1980s. Based on the insight that selling toys is not affected by cultural differences and that people will buy toys even if the economy is down, the Woo family started ABC Toys in a warehouse district in downtown Los Angeles in 1979. They imported toys from warehouses in their native Hong Kong and wholesaled toys to flea market vendors and swap meet retailers. As business boomed, the Woos bought buildings around Fourth and Wall Streets, filling them with Chinese and Sino-Vietnamese tenants. The Woos encouraged the tenants to get into the wholesale toy business. As a result, the "Toy District" was born. In 1989, the Woos spun off a second enterprise, Megatoys, on Second Street. Within a year, they doubled the family's sales to $30 million. In 1998, the annual sales of Megatoys exceeded $30 million with more than 100 wholesale businesses as tenants in the buildings that the Woo family own.

除了以上華裔商界的新生代領導人，華人也是洛市城中玩具批發業擴展的重要領導力量

**玩具製造業　　Mega Toys**

一心曾想成爲物理博士的胡澤群，以及曾是香港股票經紀的胡德群兄弟二人，在洛市開創了上億元的玩具生意，並在一九八零年代將洛杉磯提昇爲太平洋地區貿易的全國樞紐。胡氏兄弟認爲玩具生意不受文化異同的影響，即使在經濟不景氣時，人們也會購買玩具，便毅然投入。胡家在一九七九年先從洛市中心批發區的ABC玩具公司開始，由故鄉－香港的批發商處，進口玩具，再將玩具賣給本地跳蚤市場的零售商人。當生意漸有起色，即在四街和華爾街交口處買下一座樓房，租給華裔和越華裔，並鼓勵他們從事批發玩具的行業，玩具區也就因此而逐漸形成。一九八九年，胡氏又開展了另一實業 — 二街上的Megatoys。僅在一年內，銷售額即加倍成長達三千萬元。一九九八年，Megatoys的年度業績超過三千萬元，胡氏家族在玩具區擁有的樓房裡就有一百多家從事玩具批發的租戶。

▶ **Political Representation**

The presence of large number of Asian immigrants has had a significant impact on Los Angeles' economy, politics, education, culture, social services and intergroup relations. In the California presidential primary election in March 2000, 45% of Asian voters identified themselves as Democrats. The dramatic increase in the Chinese-American population in Los Angeles also has helped Chinese Americans move into electoral politics as members of school boards, city councils, state legislatures and even Congress. Mayors of several cities with major Chinese-American populations have appointed Chinese Americans as city officials. Many of these political campaigns relied on mailers written in Chinese and other Asian languages, making major strides toward acceptance in mainstream politics. Today there are ten Chinese Americans serving as city council members and eleven Chinese Americans serving on school boards.

**華人參政**

亞裔移民對洛縣的經濟、政治、教育、文化、社會服務和族裔關係有相當大的影響。二千年三月份的總統初選中，有百分之四十五的亞裔選民表示爲民主黨人。洛杉磯華裔人口的急速增加也使華人得以經選舉進入學區教委會、市議會、州議會和國會。在一些華裔人口佔相當比例的城市，市長已指派華人出任高層政府官員。許多競選活動也採用中文和其他亞裔文字進行宣傳，華裔爲求主流社會接納已跨出一大步。目前，華裔已有十人獲選爲市議員，另有十一人進入學區教委會。

▶ **City council members are include:**

Wen Chang of Diamond Bar, Judy Chu of Monterey Park, Michael Gin of Redondo Beach, Grace Hu of Cerritos, Joaquin Lim of Walnut, Dolly Leong of Rosemead, Carol Liu of La Canada-Flintridge, Julie Sa of Fullerton, Ben Wong of West Covina, Paul Zee of South Pasadena and Sheng Chang of Arcadia.

**市議員**

鑽石吧市張文生，蒙市趙美心，麗浪多海灘市甄家偉，喜瑞都市胡張燕燕，胡桃市林恩成、柔似蜜市Dolly Leong，拉卡尼達弗林楚奇的劉璿卿，富樂頓市 Julie Sa，西柯汶納市黃思寧，和南帕莎迪納市徐惠城。

Matthew Fong was elected as California Treasurer in 1995. During his four-year term, he launched an aggressive campaign to make California the financial and commercial center of the Pacific Rim. Fong ran an unsuccessful campaign for senator in November 1998.

一九九四年，鄺傑靈當選加州財務長，在四年任內期間，他積極展開工作，將加州發展為太平洋的金融和商業中心。一九九八年十一月，鄺傑靈競選聯邦參議員失利。

Photo courtesy of Matthew Fong

## ▶ School boards members are include:

Joseph Chang and Norman Hsu of Hacienda La Puente Unified School District, Olympia Chen of ABC United School District, Victor King of Glendale Community College Board of Trustees, David Lau of Garvey School District, York Lee of Walnut Unified School District, David Leong of Rosemead School District, Becky Ung of San Marino United School District, Sophie Wong of Alhambra School District, Julia Wu of Los Angeles Community College District and Melody Yu of Rowland Unified School District.

### 學區教育委員

哈仙達拉朋地學區的徐乃星和張，ABC學區的Olympia Chen，格蘭岱爾社區大學校董Victor King，嘉偉學區劉達強，胡桃學區李安岳，柔似密學區劉達強，聖瑪利諾學區吳雷洛美，阿罕布拉學區黃趙企晨，洛杉磯社區大學校董吳黎耀華，和羅蘭崗學區王小如。

▶ In June of 1998, Matthew Fong, former California State Treasurer, won the Republican Party primary for U.S. Senator. He was, however, defeated by Democrat Barbara Boxer in the general election in November. Fong is the son of the former California Secretary of State March Fong Eu, the first Chinese-American woman elected to the state legislature and the current U.S. Ambassador to Micronesia.

In the judicial branch arena, Chinese Americans have broken new ground given that there was a time in California history when people of Chinese ancestry could not serve on juries or even testify in court. Despite the social and legal obstacles they have faced, Chinese Americans have sustained a very high level of professional excellence and dedication to public service. Prominent judges include: California Court of Appeal Judge Elwood Lui, California Supreme Court Judges Joyce Kennard and Ming William Chin, Federal District Judge Ronald Lew, and County Superior Court Judge Rose Hum.

一九九八年六月，加州財務長鄺傑靈獲共和黨提名競選聯邦參議員，但不幸在十一月大選時，敗給民主黨的對手芭芭拉·鮑克塞。鄺傑靈是前加州州務卿余江月桂之子，余女士為全美第一位州級民選代表，她目前獲派出使密克羅西亞大使。

在司法的領域內，華人也開創出新天地，華人在加州曾無法擔任陪審員或是在法庭上作證。雖然面對社會和法律的障礙，華人一直保持專業，並在社會服務方面克盡心力。傑出的法官有加州上訴法院法官Elwood Lui，加州最高法院法官Joyce Kennard和陳惠明，聯邦法官劉成威及洛縣最高法院法官Rose Hum。

## ▶ Chinese American Students

The educational achievements of Los Angeles Chinese community have been spectacular, far surpassing those of whites. Chinese Los Angelenos are twice as likely as whites to have one or more college degrees. An estimated 41 percent of the Chinese population, compared to 22 percent of the white population have completed four or more years of college.

Students of Asian descent make up the largest ethnic group among undergraduates at UC Riverside, UC Irvine and UCLA. Among the Asian students, Chinese represents the largest ethnic group. Asian students represent 47% of all students in UC Irvine, and close to 40% in UCLA and UC Riverside. Chinese-American students are playing key roles in student government, university publications and other organizations. They are redefining the image of a typical UC student and creating new norms for California's most prestigious public universities.[8]

The dramatic increase in the number and proportion of Chinese-American students has influenced curricula and academic programs in many colleges and universities. Under pressure from the increased number of Chinese-American students, many universities have established Asian-American study programs and offer Asian-American courses and majors. In the area of curriculum selection, Asians often dominate science related majors.

In the past, as with all other non-white minorities, Chinese students were not represented in proportion to their population. Chinese Americans accused many of the nation's top universities such as UCLA of discriminating against applicants of Chinese descent. But the public would no longer tolerate a public university system that did not reflect the state's diverse population. As a result, affirmative action and quota systems were implemented to provide Asians and other minorities with opportunities in higher education. Ironically, today students of Asian descent make up 30% of UC's enrollment, but only 10% of the state's total population. UCI has been sarcastically been called the "University of Chinese Immigrants", and UCLA referred to as the "University of Caucasians Lost among Asians." From the point of view of other ethnic groups, Asians may have an unfair advantage. In some way they have become a victim of their own success. Chinese and whites alike have become the victims of what some call "reverse discrimination". It remains to be seen what will be worked out in the diversity controversy. With the incredible cultural diversity in Los Angeles, controversies like this certainly will not disappear in the near future.

The future Museum of Chinese American History will be located on the north bay of Los Angeles Street and Arcadia Avenue, in the El Pueblo de Los Angeles Historical Monument. The Garnier Building is the only remaining building from Old Chinatown, as well as one of the oldest existing Chinese commercial structures in California.

華人歷史博物館未來將座落在洛杉磯街北和亞凱迪街的El Pueblo de洛杉磯歷史紀念碑。加尼爾大樓是舊中國城僅存的樓宇，也是加州最老的華商建築物之一。

Photo courtesy of the El Pueblo de Los Angeles Historical Monument, Museum of Chinese American History Collection

寂寞的辮子

## 華裔學生

洛縣華人在教育界的成就斐然，遠超過白人。華人中有大學學位的人數是大約是白人的兩倍，大約有百分之四十一的華人完成四年大學教育或更高學位，白人則只有百分之二十二。

在河濱縣加大、爾灣加大和洛杉磯加大的大學部，亞裔學生人數最多，而在亞裔學生中，華裔學生又佔最大多數。爾灣加大有百分之四十七的學生是亞裔，洛杉磯加大和河濱縣加大的亞裔學生接近百分之四十，華裔學生在學生組織、校園社團、大學刊物和其他組織都扮演著重要角色，亞裔學生們正在塑造加大學生的新形象，同時也為加州公立大學系統開創新局面。[8]

華裔學生人數激增連帶影響許多大學的課程和教學計劃。在華裔學生人數日益增加的壓力下，許多加大系統和其他主要的美國大學紛紛開設亞美研究計劃，也開辦亞美科系，提供許多亞美相關課程。

在過去，與其他非白人族裔的學生一般，華裔的大學入學人數與全人口的結構不成比例，華裔學生控訴如UCLA的名校歧視華裔申請學生，而社會大眾也再無法容忍大學系統不反映全州人口多元現實的情形。結果，平權法案與配額系統雙管齊下，以保障亞裔與其他少數族裔的工作和教育機會，然而，諷刺的是，加大有百分之三十的亞裔學生，但亞裔只佔全州百分之十的人口。爾灣加大被稱為華裔移民大學，洛杉磯加大被稱為白人迷失在亞裔中的大學。在其他族裔的眼中，亞裔可能得到不公平的優勢，但在其他方面，又因為多方面的成功而受傷害，華裔和白人一般，竟成為反族裔歧視的受害者，在各方的爭議中，未來發展仍不可知。洛杉磯的多元文化交融方興未艾，如是的爭議在可見的未來恐難停歇。

Chinese Historical Society of Southern California celebrated the contributions of Chinese American World War II veterans at its Fall Dinner, held on Nov. 10. 1994

參加二次大戰的華裔退伍軍人於一九九四年十一月十日聚會，慶祝二次大戰結束五十週年。

Photo courtesy of Johnny Yee.

The founder and leader of "Immortals" Jeff Chan
with his children Vince and Jennifer showcase their
Chinese lion dance performance at the Bower
Museum in Santa Ana. Immortals has participated
in many spectacular events and movies including
the 1984 Los Angeles Summer Olympic, "The
Replacement Killers", musical video "Mulan", etc.

"Immortals"的創辦人和領導人Jeff Chan與其子女
Vince和Jennifer在聖塔安納的鮑爾博物館表演舞
獅。Immortals經常在許多電影和活動中表演，如
一九八四年洛杉磯夏季奧運、電影「The
Replacement Killers」和「木蘭」

Photo courtesy of Jeff Chan.

Chinese Historical Society of Southern
California has been the leading group in
the Annual Golden Dragon New Year
Parade in Chinatown, 1998.

南加州華人歷史學會爲一九九八年中國
新年金龍遊行對伍中的前導團體。

Photo courtesy of Johnny Yee.

寂寞的辮子

### Chinese language school

The Southern California Council of Chinese Schools has a membership of more than 100 Chinese language schools with over 20,000 students. Of the 100 schools, Irvine, Cerritos, San Marino and Torrance are the largest. Thirty to forty percent are concentrated in the San Gabriel Valley. Many independent schools are run by local churches, temples and cultural associations. One example, the San Fernando Valley Chinese Cultural Association runs a Chinese language school with more than 500 students on Saturday. It offers a wide range of Chinese language classes for academic credit in Los Angeles public schools. Its teachers have contributed significantly to the method and scope of Chinese language curriculum as well as the SAT II testing. Some Chinese-American children attend Chinese schools after regular school hours or on the weekends to learn to read and write the Chinese language

### 中文學校

南加州有超過一百多所中文學校，共有兩萬多名學生，其中爾灣、喜瑞都、聖瑪利諾和托侖斯是南加州最大的中文學校，有百分之三十到四十的中文學校集中在聖蓋博谷。許多中文學校由教會、寺廟或文化中心斥資興建，如聖弗南度谷中華文化協會所創辦的週末中文學校即有五百多名學童，所授之中文課程並獲洛杉磯公立學校承認學分，中文學校也提供SAT II 測驗的輔導課程。有些華裔學生在課後和週末到中文學校上課，學習讀寫中文。

Celena and Crystal Smith dressed in traditional Chinese costume with their grandfather Tang Yu Choi on a Chinese New Year parade float in February 2000. The children study the Chinese language and are an example of how East meets West in Los Angeles.

史慧玲與史慧晶穿著中國傳統服飾和祖父鄧汝才攝於二千年二月，一輛參加中國新年遊行的花車前。孩子們在中文學校學中文，正是洛衫磯東西文化兼容並蓄的寫照。

Photo courtesy of Icy Smith

The Monterey Park Plaza on Garvey Boulevard, 1999.

一九九九年的嘉偉大道上的Monterey Park Plaza。

Photo courtesy of Michael S. Smith

One of Chinese retail malls along Valley Boulevard, 1999.

一九九九年，山谷大道上的華人購物中心。

Photo courtesy of Michael S. Smith

寂寞的辮子

## ▶ Assimilation and Acculturation

Many Chinese Americans have been, and continue to move in the direction of acculturation. As Chinese children attend suburban schools, becoming more competent in English than in Chinese, they are beginning to view themselves as more American than Chinese. The majority of second- and third- generation Chinese Americans have already lost their native language and many cultural traditions.

No matter how Americanized they become, and how similar to whites in values, aspirations or social lifestyles, Chinese Americans will sometimes be perceived as different, and subjected to cultural stereotypes and social injustice. Therefore, ethnic identity and consciousness among Chinese Americans are not likely to disappear entirely.

## 同化

許多華人現已逐漸朝同化的方向前進，華人子弟在學校上課，英文能力比中文更好，孩子們也漸漸自我認同為美國人，而非華人。大多數第二代和第三代華人已經遺忘了母語和許多傳統的文化。

無論他們美國化的程度，或是價值觀、期望、態度和行為與白人愈趨接近，華人由於膚色，有時還是會被認為是不同的一群。因此，華裔的族裔認知不可能完全消失。

# ▶ The Future

Today generations of Chinese Americans have successfully integrated into almost every walk of life and in almost every part of Southern California. And a new trend is being realized with Chinese and other ethnic groups in the region. Instead of entering into a melting pot, some communities are predominantly ethnic by choice, creating the salad bowl effect. With the influence of racism less prevalent in today's society, expressing one's cultural identity is often not only accepted, but something celebrated. The convenience for shopping, working and entertainment all within a cultural umbrella is remarkable. Areas such as the communities in the San Gabriel Valley are more like Taiwan or Hong Kong than other American cities. Some say the world's top Chinese restaurants are no longer in Asia, but in places like Monterey Park. Knowledge of English is not necessary for many jobs in these communities and local services offered by civic organizations are often better than they are in American society as a whole. One can work, play and live comfortably with only a Chinese cultural experience. In recent years, communities such as Irvine have experienced a demographic shift with Chinese Americans as a major component, drawn by high-tech jobs and top-rated schools.

However, this modern version of ethnic groups having their own communities may lead to a Balkanization. In the event of an economic downturn, the various cultural groups may find each other as scapegoats, with clashes inevitable. The ethnic mix in Los Angeles is like no other place, and the future could bring the best or the worst scenario. The horrible experience of Korean storeowners during the civil unrest of 1992 was a result of criminals of course, but cultural and economic factors may have played a more important role.

At the dawn of the new millennium with unprecedented economic growth in the country, racism against Chinese has not disappeared with the end of the Chinese Exclusion Act of 1882. Wen Ho Lee, a nuclear scientist who pled guilty to mishandling secret information, had 58 of 59 felony counts against him dropped. After a controversial and many say "racist public campaign" against him, U.S. District Judge James Parker apologized to him for his nine months of incarceration, and let him out with time served. Later, the New York Times admitted that it had adopted the sense of alarm, and said that Lee may have been only a minor player, or completely uninvolved. Experiences like this have raised concerns on cultural and political loyalties among many Chinese Americans.[9]

Nevertheless, few would like to return to a time where the struggle of making a new life was so overwhelmingly difficult. Remembering the early history of discrimination and racism against Chinese Americans in Los Angeles is critically important, "those not remembering the past are condemned to repeat it". But on the more optimistic side, for the most part, the region has proven to be an example of how diverse people can live together peacefully. In fact, the greater Los Angeles area is likely to be what the rest of the world will look like 20 years from now.

Today, Chinese Americans are making great strides in the arts and humanities, science and technology, sports and the entertainment industries. Countless success stories are testament. Some examples include writer Amy Tan, journalist Connie Chung, playwright and producer David Henry Hwang, Academy Award-winning filmmakers James Wong Howe, film director Ang Lee, top entertainment executives Christopher Lee and Teddy Zee, Olympic and World figure-skating medallist Michelle Kwan, medical doctor and AIDS researcher David Ho, astronaut scientist Taylor Wang, engineer and entrepreneur William Mow and many others.

The history of Chinese people in Los Angeles has been long and fascinating. The future will certainly be no less remarkable. The high level of enrollment of Chinese Americans in high-tech studies programs in universities will ensure a continued contribution to science and the technical industries. With the emergence of China in the global marketplace, the 400,000 Chinese American residents of Southern California will become an increasingly important link to the East. For certain, the future of Chinese Americans in Los Angeles will be nothing like the past, but the lonely miners, the railroad coolies, the laundry and restaurant owners of the past must never be forgotten.

# 未來

今日的在美華人幾乎已成功的融入南加的各個生活層面。而在華裔和其他少數族裔的社區裡，一種新興的趨勢正衍生開來，不同與以往強調的大熔爐效應，有些社區標榜族裔色彩，形成一種沙拉碗的風貌。在現今的社會中，種族歧視已漸式微，表現個人和文化的特質反而受到大眾的接受和鼓舞。在屬於個人的文化區域內購物、工作、享受娛樂已漸成流行。如聖蓋博谷已如同台、港城市，不似傳統的美國城市。甚至人稱世界頂級的中國餐館不在亞洲，而在蒙特利公園市。在這些社區裡謀職，英語對某些工作已非必要，若干民眾團體所提供的服務也較傳統美國社會為佳。一般人可以在華裔文化的環境中輕鬆工作、娛樂和生活，怡然自得。近年來，如爾灣一般的社區已經歷人口結構的改變，由於高科技工作和優秀學區的吸引，華人已漸成社區主流。

然而，現今的族裔自成社區可能導致社區孤立，一旦經濟疲軟，各社區交相指責恐在所難免。洛杉磯的族裔混合舉世無雙，未來的榮衰實難逆料。一九九三年韓國城暴亂的恐怖經驗雖導因於犯罪事件，但文化和經濟因素也助長了暴動情勢的升高。

千禧年初，全國正享受著前所未有的經濟榮景，然而，對華裔的族裔歧視並未隨著一八八二年排華法案的廢止而消失。針對華裔核子科學家李文和不當處理機密文件的五十九項重罪指控，在他就其中一項認罪後，其他五十八項即被撤銷，社區一片譁然，並有許多人認為李文和不過就是族裔歧視的另一名受害者，美國聯邦法官James Parker 對長達九個月的羈押向李文和致歉，並予折抵刑期。稍後，紐約時報也承認過份渲染報導，並稱李文和可能在洩密案中無足輕重，甚至完全無關。類似事件再次引發對華人的文化與政治忠誠度的關切。[9]

鮮少有人願意回想過去劈荊斬棘、胼手胝足的艱苦歲月，但記取洛杉磯華人早期受到歧視的歷史卻格外重要，古語有云：「記取教訓方能免於重蹈覆轍。」但樂觀來看，洛杉磯也驗證了多元族裔可和睦共處的事實，大洛杉磯地區可堪為全世界其他地區未來二十年的寫照。

今日，華裔在人文藝術、科技、體育、娛樂等各方面大顯身手，無數成功的故事傳為中外美談，如作家譚恩美、記者鍾毓華、劇作家黃哲倫、奧斯卡金像獎得主王家衛、李安、娛樂界名人Christopher Lee和Teddy Zee、奧林匹克和世界花式溜冰好手關穎珊、抗愛滋症研究醫學博士何大一、太空人王贛駿和企業家毛昭寰等。

洛杉磯華人的歷史淵遠流長而令人震撼，未來發展更將尤有甚之。華人在各大學科學和高科技計劃的參與將持續為科學和科技界做出貢獻。中國在全球市場上崛起，南加四十萬華人為連繫遠東憑添助力而更形重要。可以肯定的是，洛杉磯華人的實力絕不容小覷，但孤苦的礦工、鐵路工、洗衣店和餐館老闆將永遠不會被遺忘。

寂寞的辮子

The 560,000 square-foot San Gabriel Square is the largest retail complex in the San Gabriel Valley. It is comprised of 100 stores, anchored by a leading Chinese Tawa Supermarket and a department store, 1999.

佔地五十六萬平方呎的聖蓋博廣場是聖蓋博谷最大的零售購物中心，共有一百家商店，大華超市和一樣百貨公司是商場內的主要店家。

Photo courtesy of Michael S. Smith

**Chronology  大事記**

1848   The discovery of gold in Sutter's Mill sets off a large wave of immigration from China.
在Sutter's Mill發現金礦，大批華裔移民開始渡海而來。

1850   Census recorded first two Chinese servants, Ah Fou and Ah Luce in Los Angeles.
人口普查顯示洛杉磯有兩名華裔僕役，名叫阿福和阿祿

1854   California Supreme Court upholds laws that prohibit people of color from testifying against whites.
加州最高法院立法禁止有色族裔在法庭上作不利於白人的證辭。

1863   Recruiting begins in China to bring thousands of laborers to work on the Central Pacific Railroad.
開始自中國大陸招募人工以修築中央太平洋鐵路。

1868   The Sino-American Treaty is signed, allowing Chinese immigration for "purposes of curiosity, trade, or permanent residence" but restricting the right of Chinese people to become naturalized U.S. citizens.
中美條約簽署，允許華裔為觀光、經商或永久居留美國而移民，但不得歸化為美國公民。

1869   Chinese laborers come to the San Fernando Valley to work on a road construction project
華工抵舊金山，開始修築鐵路。

1870   The Naturalization Act excludes Chinese people from becoming U.S. citizens and prohibits wives of Chinese laborers from entering the United States.
排華的移民法禁止華人歸化為公民，並禁止華工妻子來美。

1871   The infamous Chinese Massacre takes place. A mob of 500 white and Mexican Angelenos kills 19 innocent Chinese and loots Negro Alley in the Chinese quarter.
不為人知的華人大屠殺發生。一群五百多人的白人和墨裔殺死十九名無辜華人，在華人聚居的黑人巷大肆劫掠。

1876   The Southern Pacific rail link connecting San Francisco and Los Angeles is completed. Chinese labor is instrumental in completing the perilous 7,000-foot San Fernando Tunnel. Hundreds of Chinese railroad workers move to Los Angeles upon completion of the rail line, fueling increased anti-Chinese sentiment in Los Angeles.
南太平洋鐵路連接舊金山和洛杉磯一段完工。華工對長達七千呎的舊金山隧道貢獻極大。數百名鐵路工人在鐵路完工後遷來洛杉磯，洛杉磯日漸升高的排華情緒一觸即發。

1876   The first Chinese Presbyterian Church is established (presently known as True Light Chinese Presbyterian Church) at San Pedro and First Streets.
第一所華人長老會成立(現名為眞光華人長老會)，教會址在聖彼卓和一街口。

1882   The Chinese Exclusion Act is passed, suspending most immigration from China for ten years. It was the first time in U.S. history in which legislation denied admission to a particular ethnic group.
第一宗排華法案通過，十年內禁止大多數來自中國的華人入美。這是美國史上首度立法將移民分等，決定是否給予移民許可。

1886   Construction of the San Gabriel Railroad results in clashes between Chinese and white railroad workers; white railroad workers attack and burn several Chinese laundries in Pasadena.
華工與白人在修築聖蓋博鐵路時衝突，白人鐵路工人在帕莎迪納攻擊華人，焚燒華人洗衣店。

1887   Original Chinese quarter is burned by arsonist. Buildings are quickly replaced by new construction near the Plaza.
華商聚集的角落被縱火燒毀，新樓房很快完工。

1890   The Chinese Consolidated Benevolent Association is formed in the Garnier Building to advocate political and social advancement for the Chinese community.
中華會館在加尼爾大樓創辦，領導華人社區的政治和社會進步。

1892 The Geary Act is passed, requiring Chinese laborers to register with the Federal government or face deportation.
蓋瑞法案通過，華工必須向聯邦政府登記，否則將被驅逐出境。

1893 Chinese are expelled from Cahuenga Valley by local citizens. Similar expulsions occur in Norwalk, Burbank, Vernon and Pasadena.
華人被本地人驅離出卡宏加谷，諾瓦克、勃班克、佛能、帕莎迪納也發生類似事情。

1894 Chinese are invited for the first time to participate in the Fiesta de las Flores parade in Los Angeles.
華人首次受邀參加洛市Fiesta de las Flores遊行。

1895 The first Chinese Children's School is founded at 766 Juan Street.
第一所華人子弟學校於766 Juan Street創校。

1898 The first Chinese newspaper, Wah Mei Sun Po, is founded by Ng Poon Chew.
第一份中文報紙華美新報由Poon Chew Ng創辦。

1902 Congress extends indefinitely the Chinese Exclusion Act, prohibiting the Chinese from immigration.
國會通過無限期排華法案，禁止華裔移民。

1909 Louie Quan builds the City Market wholesale produce terminal. The City Market is to become a vital element in the economy of the Los Angeles Chinese community, and also becomes the focal point of a separate Chinese commercial and residential community apart from Chinatown.
Louie Quan建造市集蔬果批發站。市集成為洛杉磯華人經濟重鎮，也是華埠以外華商和華人集會的所在。

1912 The Los Angeles Lodge of the Chinese American Citizens Alliance in San Francisco is founded to promote civil rights of Chinese Americans. The name is changed in 1915 to its present name of the Chinese American Citizen Alliance.
源自舊金山的同源會在洛杉磯成立分會，致力提升華人權益，一九一五年改為現名。

1923 You Chung Hong becomes the first Chinese American to practice law in Southern California. For 50 years, Chinese Americans regard Hong as the country's foremost Chinese attorney based on his relentless work to repeal the Chinese Exclusion Act of 1882.
洪耀宗成為第一位在南加州執業的華裔律師，五十多年來，由於他在一八八二年領導推翻排華法案，是公認最傑出的華人律師。

1924 A second Exclusion Act prevents immigration for Chinese who do not have at least a master's degree.
第二次排華法案出現，除非具碩士學位，否則不得移民美國。

1931 Mei Wah Club, a social and athletic organization for Chinese-American women, is founded.
華裔婦女社交活動的組織 —美華會成立。

1932 The Cable Act is passed, decreeing that U.S. born Chinese American women marrying foreign-born Asians automatically lose their citizenship.
Cable法案通過，規定在美出生的華裔婦女若與外國出生的亞裔成婚，將失去公民身份。

1933 Old Chinatown is condemned and razed to make way for the new Union Station.
舊中國城被拆遷以興建聯合車站。

1938 China City and New Chinatown open in the month of June within three weeks of each other.
中國市和新中國城在六月份相隔三週先後開放。

1941 China and the United States become political allies. Many Chinese Americans enter the armed forces.
中美結為政治盟邦。許多在美華人加入陸軍。

1942　World War II is a turning point for Chinese Americans. About 12,000 are drafted or enlisted. The American Women's Voluntary Service (AWVS) Chinese Center is formed by a group of Chinese-American women to support war relief activities.
二次世界大戰爲華人轉捩點。大約有一萬二千華人接受徵召。一群華裔婦女組織美華婦女志願服務中心，支持救災活動。

1943　The Chinese Exclusion Act passed in 1882 is finally repealed, ending a 61-year ban on Chinese entering the U.S. , and finally ending a life of bachelorhood for many single men. Chinese descendants are now eligible for admission under quota laws.
一八八二年通過的排華法案終於被廢止，結束了六十一年的排華歷史，終於結束了許多華裔男子的單身歲月，華人可依配額取得移民許可。

1945　The War Brides Act is passed, allowing approximately 6,000 Chinese women to enter the United States as brides of men in the U.S. armed forces.
制定戰爭新娘法案，允許六千華人婦女入境美國，與美國陸軍軍人成婚。

1945　Los Angeles Chinese Post 628 is formed to provide readjustment assistance to returning World War II Chinese-American veterans.
洛衫磯第628軍團成立，協助二次大戰後華裔退役軍人重返社會。

1948　The United States Supreme Court rules that real estate deed restrictions prohibiting the sale of property to racial minorities is unconstitutional.
最高法院判定，禁止少數族裔購置房地產爲違憲。

1949　A second disastrous fire demolished the main section of China City.
第二次大火燒毀了中國市的主要地區。

1952　The Immigration and Nationality Act is passed, granting the rights of naturalization and eventual citizenship for foreign-born Asians with a quota of 105 immigrants per year for each Asian country.
移民和國籍法案通過，每年允許在亞洲出生的移民，每一國家一百零五名移民歸化配額。

1953　The Refugee Relief Act, expiring at the end of 1956, allows Chinese political refugees to come to the United States.
援助難民法案允許華裔政治難民來美，該法案於一九五六年終止。

1953　The remainder of Old Chinatown is completely torn down for the construction of the Hollywood/Santa Ana Freeway.
僅存的舊中國城被完全拆毀，以建造好萊塢/聖塔安納公路。

1955　The Chinese Chamber of Commerce of Los Angeles is established to promote and encourage the development of the Chinese-American business community.
羅省中華總商會成立，致力促進華商社區的繁榮和發展。

1959　Judge Delbert Wong is the first Chinese American appointed as judge in the continental United States. The appointment was recognized as an historic event, receiving national media attention.
黃錦紹法官成爲第一位獲任命的華人法官。此項任命被視爲歷史記錄，獲媒體注意。

1962　Cathay Bank, the first Chinese-American bank in Southern California, is founded to provide and promote economic development of the Chinatown community.
南加州第一家華資銀行—國泰銀行創辦，促進華埠社區的經濟發展。

1965　Discriminatory immigration laws end, opening up U.S. immigration to Asian countries. The new immigration law sets a new quota of 20,000 persons from any country.
歧視移民法終結，打開亞洲國家移民美國之道。新移民法給予每個國家兩萬人配額。

1970　New waves of Chinese immigrants move to Monterey Park, the first suburban Chinatown.
新移民潮湧進蒙特利公園，在郊區創造了一個中國城。

1974 March Fong Eu is elected as California Secretary of State with a record-setting three million votes.
余江月桂以破記錄的三百萬選票當選加州州務卿。

1975 The end of U.S. military action in Southeast Asia results in large-scale immigration of Vietnamese, Laotian and Cambodian refugees to Los Angeles, many of whom are of Chinese descent.
美國在東南亞的軍事行動結束，大批來自越、棉、寮的難民進入洛杉磯，其中有許多是華裔。

1977 Frederic Hsieh promotes Monterey Park as the "Chinese Beverly Hills" in Chinese newspapers throughout Hong Kong and Taiwan, accounting for a large influx of Chinese immigrants to Monterey Park.
謝叔綱在港台的煤體上，將蒙特利公園比喻為華人的比佛利山，吸引大批華裔移民遷入蒙特利公園市。

1978 Dr. Daniel Wong is the first Chinese American elected to the Cerritos City Council. He served the city for 14 years, including two terms as mayor.
黃錦波成為第一位當選喜瑞都市議會的華裔市議員。他任職市議會達十四年，其中擔任兩屆市長，一九八三年，他成為全美第一位華裔市長，一九八零年，黃錦波領導加州華人支持雷根。

1980 The Chinatown Redevelopment Project is adopted to promote Chinatown as a cultural and commercial center.
華埠重建計劃展開，重整華埠為一文化商業中心。

1980 The Refugee Act is signed into law by President Jimmy Carter, enabling more refugees to enter Los Angeles.
卡特總統在任內簽署難民法案，使更多難民得以進入洛杉磯。

1980 As a result of an announcement that they would add a Chinese language page to their newspapers, the Monterey Park Progress and Alhambra Post-Advocate become victims of vandalism and hate mail.
蒙特利公園前進報和阿罕布拉先鋒報因對外宣佈將增加中文新聞版，成了仇恨郵件和惡意攻擊的對象。

1981 The U.S. Immigration and Naturalization Service grants Taiwan a separate immigration quota to facilitate family reunifications.
美國移民局允台灣個別移民配額，方便移民家庭團聚。

1981 Justice Elwood Lui is appointed to the California Court of Appeal, becoming the first Chinese American State Appellate Court judge.
Elwood Lui法官獲聯邦上訴法院任命，成為全美第一位華裔上訴法院法官。

1984 Lily Lee Chen becomes the first Chinese-American woman mayor in the continental United States. As mayor of Monterey Park, she encourages Chinese business owners to put up multilingual signs.
陳李婉若成為全美第一位民選女性華裔市長。在擔任蒙特利公園市市長期間，她提倡華商懸掛雙語商招。

1985 Monterey Park is named an "All American City" by the National Municipal League and USA Today for its effective citizenship and significant civic accomplishments brought about through a blending of private and public efforts.
蒙特利公園市在市府與民間的合作下，公民表現傑出，獲全美城市聯盟和今日美國提名為「全美模範城市」。

1985 Michael Woo is the first Asian American elected to the Los Angeles City Council. He later runs a strong, though unsuccessful, campaign for mayor of Los Angeles in 1993.
胡紹基成為第一位洛市民選華裔市議員，他在一九八三年時積極投入洛市市長選舉，不幸落選。

1985 Dr. Taylor Wang, a Chinese American physicist, becomes the second Asian American in space when he flies aboard the Challenger.
華人物理學家王贛駿博士登上挑戰者號太空梭，成為第二位亞裔太空人。

The Lonely Queue

1986 Monterey Park is identified as "the first suburban Chinatown" in the United States.
蒙特利公園被視爲第一個在郊區的中國城。

1987 Judge Ronald Lew is the first Chinese American to be appointed to the U.S. District Court.
劉成威成爲第一位華裔聯邦法院法官。

1989 Justice Joyce Kennard becomes the first judge of Chinese ancestry to be appointed to the California Supreme Court.
Joyce Kennard法官成爲第一位華裔加州最高法院法官。

1990 The Chinese Memorial Shrine in historic Evergreen Cemetery is designated as Los Angeles Historic Cultural Monument No. 486 on August 31.
八月三十一日，長青墓園內的華人紀念堂被設計爲第486號洛杉磯歷史文化碑。

1990 Sophie Wong is the first Chinese-American woman to be elected to the Alhambra School Board
黃趙企晨成爲第一位阿罕布拉學區華裔教委。

1992 The Chinese Historical Society of Southern California purchases the Chinese Memorial Shrine for $14,000 to preserve the endangered monument on September 17.
南加州華人歷史學會在九月十七日以一萬四千元買下華人紀念堂，以保存頹圮的紀念碑。

1992 Dr. Judy Chu is elected as the mayor of Monterey Park and re-elected in 1994.
趙美心博士當選蒙特利公園市市長，一九九四年再獲連任。

1993 David Lau is appointed to the Board of Education of Garvey School District. He is elected as the President of the Garvey School Board in 1998. In March 1999, he runs a political campaign for a seat in the Monterey Park City Council, but loses by 31 votes to his opponent. However, Lau ranks first among five Asian candidates and fourth among a total of 11 candidates.
劉達強當選嘉偉學區教委，一九九八年獲推選爲教委會主席，一九九九年三月競選蒙市市議員，以三十一票敗給對手佛列德·鮑德拉瑪，劉達強是參選的五位華人之一，得票數在十一位候選人中排名第四。

1993 Chinese American Connie Chung joins Dan Rather as co-anchor of the "CBS Evening News" and is named anchor of a prime-time news magazine, Eye to Eye with Connie Chung.
華裔鍾毓華與丹·拉瑟共同主持哥倫比亞廣播公司的晚間新聞，並在黃金時間主持一新聞雜誌節目「與鍾毓華面對面」。

1994 President Bill Clinton appoints March Fong Eu, former Secretary of State of California, to become ambassador to Micronesia.
柯林頓總統任命前加州州務卿余江月桂出使密克羅西亞。

1995 Grace Hu is elected as the **may**or of Cerritos and is re-elected in 1997.
胡張燕燕當選喜瑞都市市長，一九九七年再獲連任。

1996 Justice Ming William Chin is appointed by Governor Pete Wilson to the Supreme Court of California.
陳惠明法官獲威爾遜州長任命爲加州最高法院法官。

1996 Michele Kwan wins the Ice Skating Figure World Championship and again in 1998.
關穎珊獲世界花式溜冰冠軍，一九九八年衛冕成功。

1998 The Chinese are honored at the 47th Anniversary of the Golden Spike event at the Golden Spike National Historic Site in Promontory Summit for their contributions in helping to build the Central Pacific Railroad. A commemorative wreath is erected at the site to symbolize the lives, deaths and work of the Chinese.
在第四十七屆金釘全國紀念會中，華人因其對修築中央太平洋鐵路有功而受表揚。現場樹立起一方紀念碑，紀念華人的犧牲和貢獻。

1998 Matthew Fong wins the Republican Party primary for California Senator. However, he was defeated by his counterpart in the major election in November.
鄺傑靈代表共和黨競選聯邦參議員，在十一月大選時敗給對手。

1999 Dolly Gee is nominated by President Clinton as a federal district judge in Los Angeles.
Dolly Gee 獲總統柯林頓提名爲洛衫磯聯邦法院法官。

1999 The Chinese Historical Society of Southern California publishes a commemorative publication "Duty and Honor" to document the participation and contribution of Chinese-American World War II veterans of Southern California.
南加州華人歷史學會出版「責任和榮譽」刊物，以紀念對二次世界大戰有功的南加華人。

1999 The Chinese Chamber of Commerce of Los Angeles holds its centennial Golden Dragon Lunar New Year Parade on February 20 in Los Angeles Chinatown.
羅省中華總商會二月二十日在洛市華埠舉辦第一百年中國新年金龍大遊行和

References:
1.    Chan, David. "The Chinese in Los Angeles-A Chronology," Gum Saan Journal, July 1978, 10-12
2.    Cheng, Suellen. "Chinese Americans in Los Angeles," 1997 Los Angeles Chinese Chamber of Commerce Year Book. Los Angeles : Chinese Chamber of Commerce, 1997
3.    Asian American Almanac, Gale Research Inc. 1995.

## Footnote 附註

### Chapter 1

1.    William Mason, "The Chinese in Los Angeles," in *1976 Chinese Chamber of Commerce Souvenir Book* (Los Angeles: Chinese Chamber of Commerce, 1976), 7.
2.    "Los Angeles Chinatown-A Brief History," in *1974 Chinese Chamber of Commerce Souvenir Book* (Los Angeles: Chinese Chamber of Commerce, 1974), 1.
3.    Ibid.
4.    Laverne Mau Dicker, " *The Chinese in San Francisco: A Pictorial History,* " (New York: Dover Publication, Inc., 1979), 3.
5.    Ibid., 1.
6.    "Chinatown's Shifting Fortunes," *Los Angeles Magazine*, February 1991, 64.
7.    Dicker, *The Chinese in San Francisco*, 11.
8.    William Mason, "Chinese Fishing in Early California," in *1977 Chinese Chamber of Commerce Souvenir Book* (Los Angeles: Chinese Chamber of Commerce, 1977), 12-13.
9.    Kim Fong Tom, " *The Participation of the Chinese in the Community Life of Los Angeles,*" M.A. Thesis, University of Southern California, 1944, 15-17.
10. Wei Li, "*Spatial Transformation of an Urban Ethnic Community from Chinatown to Chinese Ethnoburb in Los Angeles,* " Dissertation, University of Southern California, 1997, 102-103.
11. "Chinatown's Shifting Fortunes," 66.
12. William Mason, "The Chinese in Los Angeles," *Los Angeles County Museum of Natural History, Museum Alliance Quarterly*, 6:2, 16
13. Margie Lew and Chuck Yee, "Whistlestop Centennial," in *1977 Chinese Chamber of Commerce Souvenir Book* (Los Angeles: Chinese Chamber of Commerce, 1977), 7-8.
14. Michael E. Engh, S.J., "A Most Excellent Field for Work: Christian Missionary Efforts in the Los Angeles Chinese Community 1870-1990," *Gum Saan Journal* (June 1992): 2-10.
15. Roberta Greenwood, "*Down by the Station: Los Angeles Chinatown 1880-1933,*" (California: University of California, Los Angeles, 1995), 20.

寂寞的辮子

16. George and Elsie Yee, "The Chinese and the Los Angeles Produce Market," *Gum Saan Journal* (December 1986): 3.

17. Greenwood, *Down by the Station*, 11.

18. "*Los Angeles Chinatown: A Brief History*," 1.

19. Greenwood, 11.

Chapter 2

1. William Mason, "The Chinese in Los Angeles," in *1976 Chinese Chamber of Commerce Souvenir Book* (Los Angeles: Chinese Chamber of Commerce, 1976), 9-10

2. Roberta Greenwood, "*Down by the Station: Los Angeles Chinatown 1880-1933*," (California: University of California, Los Angeles, 1995), 23.

3. Otis Wiles, "War of Great Chinese Tongs," *Los Angeles Times*, January 16, 1921, Part II, p.1.

4. Lucie Cheng and Suellen Cheng, "*Chinese Women of Los Angeles*," in *Linking Our Lives* (Los Angeles, Chinese Historical Society of Southern California, 1984), 3.

5. Cecilia Rasmussen, "The City Then and Now," *Los Angeles Times*, August 30, 1993. Home Edition, M-1

6. Greenwood, *Down by the Station*, 22.

7. The information contained in this and the next three paragraphs comes from George and Elsie Yee, "The Chinese and the Los Angeles Produce Market," *Gum Saan Journal* (December 1986): 5-8.

8. Greenwood, 18-19.

9. Cheng, Chinese Women of Los Angeles, 7.

10. Y.C. Hong, "Milestones of the Chinese-American Citizens Alliance," in t*he Chinese American Citizens Alliance 80th Anniversary Yearbook* (Los Angeles: Chinese American Citizens Alliance, 1992), 42-46.

Chapter 3

1. Lucie Cheng and Suellen Cheng, "Chinese Women of Los Angeles," in *Linking Our Lives* (Los Angeles, Chinese Historical Society of Southern California, 1984), 14-15.

2. Louise Leung Larson, "*Sweet Bamboo: Saga of a Chinese American Family*" (Los Angeles, Chinese Historical Society of Southern California,1989), 123-124

3. George and Elsie Yee, "The Chinese and the Los Angeles Produce Market," *Gum Saan Journal* (December 1986): 14.

4. Roberta Greenwood, "*Down by the Station: Los Angeles Chinatown 1880-1933*," (California: University of California, Los Angeles, 1995), 30.

5. " Chinese Women in California: Past and Present," *Gum Saan Journal* (May 1970): 3.

6. Ibid., 1

7. George and Elsie Yee, "The 1927 Chinese Baseball Team," *Gum Saan Journal* (December 1980): 2,5,7.

Chapter 4

1. Marjorie Lee, "Building Community," *in Linking Our Lives* (Los Angeles, Chinese Historical Society of Southern California, 1984), 93.

2. Garding Lui, "Inside Los Angeles Chinatown," (Los Angeles, 1948), 32.

3. Mary and Chuck Yee, "The Pioneer Chinese American Actors," *in 1979 Los Angeles Chinatown Souvenir Book* (Los Angeles: Chinese Chamber of Commerce), 22.

4. Ruby Ling Louie, "Reliving China City," *Gum Saan Journal* (December 1988): 2.

5. Roberta Greenwood, "*Down by the Station: Los Angeles Chinatown 1880-1933*," (California: University of California, Los Angeles, 1995), 40.

6. Cy Wong, "The Golden Years of Los Angeles Chinatown:Chinatown Landmarks," *in The Golden Years, 1938-1988* (Los Angeles, 1988), 23.

7. John Tomlinson, "Four Lives," *USC Trojan Family Magazine*, Summer 1998, 36-37.

8. Suellen Cheng and Munson Kwok, "The Golden Years of Los Angeles Chinatown," in *The Golden Years, 1938-1988* (Los Angeles, 1988), 45, 47.

9. The information contained in this and the next three paragraphs comes from Ella Yee Quan, "The Golden Years: Pioneer Families Share their History," in *The Golden Years, 1938-1988* (Los Angeles, 1988), 29-31.

10. Yukie Lee, "*Man Jen Low History*," unpublished article, 1988.

11. Marjorie Lee, "Building Community," in *Linking Our Lives* (Los Angeles, Chinese Historical Society of Southern California, 1984), 94-96.


Chapter 5

1. Louise Leung Larson, "*Sweet Bamboo: Saga of a Chinese American Family*" (Los Angeles, Chinese Historical Society of Southern California,1989)182-184

2. Garding Lui, "*Inside Los Angeles Chinatown*," (Los Angeles, 1948), 51.

3. Jim Fong, "Camaraderie for our veterans - American Legion, American-Chinese Post 628," *in Duty and Honor*, ed. Marjorie Lee (Los Angeles: Chinese Historical Society of Southern California, 1998), 28.

4. Judy Yung, "*Chinese Women of America: A Pictorial History*," (Seattle: University of Washington Press,1986), 76, 80.

5. Marjorie Lee, "Building Community," *in Linking Our Lives* (Los Angeles: Chinese Historical Society of Southern California, 1984), 98-99.

6. Lucie Cheng and Suellen Cheng, "Chinese American Women of Los Angeles," *in Linking Our Lives* (Los Angeles: Chinese Historical Society of Southern California, 1984), 18, 20.

7. Wei Li, "*Spatial Transformation of an Urban Ethnic Community from Chinatown to Chinese Ethnoburb in Los Angeles*," Dissertation, University of Southern California, 1997, 110.

8. Majorie Lee, " Coming of Age-Chinese American Women Doing their Part," *in Duty and Honor* ( Los Angeles:Chinese Historical Society of Southern California, 1998) 50,51


Chapter 6

1. Lucie Cheng and Suellen Cheng, "Chinese American Women of Los Angeles," *in Linking Our Lives* (Los Angeles: Chinese Historical Society of Southern California, 1984), 10.

2. "Los Angeles Chinese Drum and Bugle Corps," in *1978 Los Angeles Chinatown Souvenir Book* (Los Angeles: Chinese Chamber of Commerce, 1978), 59.

3. "Chinese Women in California Past and Present," in *1978 Los Angeles Chinatown Souvenir Book* (Los Angeles: Chinese Chamber of Commerce, 1978), 11.

4. "First Chinese Baptist Church of Los Angeles," in *1996 Los Angeles Chinatown Souvenir Book* (Los Angeles: Chinese Chamber of Commerce, 1996), 27.


Chapter 7

1. The information contained in this and the next paragraph comes from "Los Angeles Chinatown - A Brief History," in *1974 Chinese Chamber of Commerce Souvenir Book* (Los Angeles: Chinese Chamber of Commerce), 3.

2. "Beverly Hom and Lillian Fong, "The Golden Years of Los Angeles Chinatown : Los Angeles Chinatown 1958-1968, in *The Golden Years, 1938-1988* (Los Angeles, 1988), 55.


Chapter 8

1. Karen Lew, "The Golden Years of Los Angeles Chinatown: Chinatown : The Present," in *The Golden Years, 1938-1988* (Los Angeles, 1988), 59-60; Linda Yeung, "*Chinatown USA Profile: The Los Angeles Chapter*," (Los Angeles: Chinatown Service Center,1992), 2; Bill Sing, "Chinatown Struggles to Balance Dual Community Roles," *Los Angeles Times*, April 13, 1980.

寂寞的辮子

2. Timothy Fong, "The First Suburban Chinatown," (Philadelphia, Temple University Press, 1994), 29.

3. Ibid., 36.

4. Ibid., 49.

5. Interview by author, October 22, 1998.

6. The information contained in this and the next paragraph comes from Ibid., 69-70.

7. James B. Zazas, "*Visions of Luscombe: The Early Years*," (1993), 261; "*Reflections from 1916*," (Los Angeles: City of Monterey Park, 1996), 69.


Chapter 9

1. Linda Yeung, "*Chinatown USA Profile: The Los Angeles Chapter*," (Los Angeles: Chinatown Service Center,1992), 2.

2. Vicki Torres, "The Great Wall of Chinatown," *Los Angeles Times*, March 31, 1996, Home Edition, A-1.

3. "Old Chinatown," *Los Angeles Herald Examiner*, May 7, 1988.

4. Yeung, 3.

5. The information contained in this and the next paragraph comes from Wei Li, "*Spatial Transformation of an Urban Ethnic Community from Chinatown to Chinese Ethnoburb in Los Angeles*," Dissertation, University of Southern California, 1997, 138-142.

6. Ibid., 145.

7. Ibid., 162.

8. "City Earns All America" in *Reflections from 1916* (Los Angeles: City of Monterey Park, 1996), 49.


Chapter 10

1. Karl Schoenberger, "Breathing Life into Southland," *Los Angeles Times*, October 4, 1993, Home Edition, A-1.

2. Diane Seo, "Faded Glory," *Los Angeles Times*, November 1, 1992, p.25; Vicki Torres, "The Great Wall of Chinatown," *Los Angeles Times*, March 31, 1996, Home Edition, A-1.

3. The information contained in this and the next paragraph comes from Jill Stewart, "Forget it, Jake. It's Chinatown," *www.newtimesla.com*, March 30, 2000; George Ramos, "Seeds of Discord Grow Over Downtowns Cornfield," *Los Angeles Times*, October 21, 1999, Home Edition, B-1.

4. Douglas Young, "China Valley-The Making of an Economy Special Report," *Los Angeles Business Journal*, December 1, 1997, p.24.

5. Joel Kotkin, "California Becoming a Favorite Chinese Investment," *Los Angeles Times*, June 29, 1997, Home Edition, P. M-1.

6. Dunson Cheng, "Chinese Banks," in *1996 Los Angeles Chinatown Souvenir Book* (Los Angeles: Chinese Chamber of Commerce, 1996), 16.

7. The information contained in this and the next nine paragraphs comes from "*Hoover's Guide To The Top Southern California Companies*," Hoover's Inc.1996, 10, 13-17, 23, 112, 184, 211, 216, 242; *www.chineseinc.com/alr.htm, /kingston.htm, /bugle.htm, /viewsonic.htm*, February 3, 1999.

8. The information contained in this and the next three paragraphs comes from Diane Seo, "Growing Asian Enrollment Redefines UC Campuses," *Los Angeles Times*, December 27, 1995, Home Edition, A-1.

9. David Shaw, "New York Times Explains, Critiques Its Lee Coverage," *New York Times*, September 27, 2000, Part A, p.15.

## Selected Bibliography 參考書目

♦ Asian American Studies Center, University of California, Los Angeles, and Chinese Historical Society of Southern California. *Linking Our Lives: Chinese American Women of Los Angeles*. Los Angeles: Chinese Historical Society of Southern California, 1984.

♦ Asian American Studies Center, University of California, Los Angeles, and Chinese Historical Society of Southern California. *Origins and Destinations: 41 Essays on Chinese American*. Los Angeles: Chinese Historical Society of Southern California, 1984.

♦ Beatts, Anne. "Don't Forget Chinatown." *Los Angeles Times*, Jan. 29, 1998.

♦ Buckelew, Deborah. "Chinatown Faces Sudden Growing Pains" *Civic Center News*, July 18, 1978.

♦ Chan, David. "The Chinese in Los Angeles - A Chronology." *Gum Saan Journal* (July 1978).

♦ Chen, Sucheng. *This Bittersweet Soil: The Chinese in California Agriculture, 1860-1910*. Berkeley: University of California Press, 1986.

♦ Cheng, Dunson. "Chinese Banks." *1996 Los Angeles Chinatown Souvenir Book*. Los Angeles: Chinese Chamber of Commerce, 1996.

♦ "Chinatown's Shifting Fortunes." *Los Angeles Magazine*. February 1991.

♦ "Chinese Americans." *In Asian Americans: Contemporary Trends and Issues*. Ed. Pyong Gap Min, Thousand Oaks, California: Sage Publications, 1995.

♦ "*Chinese American Citizens Alliance 80th Anniversary Yearbook*." Los Angeles: Chinese American Citizens Alliance, 1992.

♦ "Chinese Women in California Past and Present." *1980 Los Angeles Chinatown Souvenir Book*. Los Angeles: Chinese Chamber of Commerce, 1980.

♦ Chinn, Thomas W., Him Mark Lai, and Philip P. Choy, ed. *A History of the Chinese in California: A Syllabus*. San Francisco: Chinese Historical Society of America, 1969.

♦ Dicker, Laverne Mau. *The Chinese in San Francisco: A Pictorial History*. New York: Dover Publication, Inc., 1979.

♦ Engh, Michael E. "A Most Excellent Field for Work: Christian Missionary Efforts in the Los Angeles Chinese Community, 1870-1900." *Gum Saan Journal* (June 1992).

♦ Fong, Timothy. *The First Suburban Chinatown*. Philadelphia, Temple University Press, 1994.

♦ Greenwood, Roberta. *Down By the Station: Los Angeles Chinatown 1880-1933*. California: University of California, Los Angeles, 1995.

♦ Holgan, Rick. "Ethnicity is a key factor in Assembly Democratic Primary." *Los Angeles Times*, April 21, 1994.

♦ *Hoover's Guide To The Top Southern California Companies*. Hoover's Inc. 1996.

♦ Horton, John. *The Politics of Diversity: Immigration, Resistance, and Change in Monterey Park, California*. Philadelphia: Temple University Press, 1995.

♦ Hubler, Shawn. "A Feeding Frenzy in the New Chinatown." *Los Angeles Times*, December 5, 1995.

♦ Hulse, Jerry. "Chinatown Changing as Suburbs Call Residents." *Los Angeles Times*, October 26, 1995.

♦ Kang, Connie. "Chinese in the Southland: A Changing Picture." *Los Angeles Times*, June 29, 1997

♦ Kotkin, Joel. "California Becoming a Favorite Chinese Investment." *Los Angeles Times*, June 29, 1997.

♦ Larson, Louise Leung. *Sweet Bamboo: Saga of a Chinese American Family*. Los Angeles: Chinese Historical Society of Southern California, 1989.

♦ Lew, Margie and Yee, Chuck. "Whistlestop Centennial." *1977 Chinese Chamber of Commerce Souvenir Book*. Los Angeles: Chinese Chamber of Commerce, 1977.

♦ Li, Wei. *Spatial Transformation of an Urban Ethnic Community from Chinatown to Chinese Ethnoburb in Los Angeles*." Dissertation, University of Southern California, 1997.

♦ Los Angeles Chinatown - A Brief History, *1974 Chinese Chamber of Commerce Souvenir Book*.

♦ Los Angeles: Chinese Chamber of Commerce, 1974.

♦ Lui, Garding. Inside Los Angeles Chinatown. Los Angeles, 1948.

◆ Mason, William. "Chinese Fishing In Early California." 1977 Chinese Chamber of Commerce Souvenir Book. Los Angeles: Chinese Chamber of Commerce, 1977.

-----------. "The Chinese in Los Angeles." 1976 Chinese Chamber of Commerce Souvenir Book. Los Angeles: Chinese Chamber of Commerce, 1976.

◆ McDannold, Thomas Allen. *California's Chinese Heritage: A Legacy of Places*. California: Heritage West Books, 2000.

-----------. *Development of the Los Angeles Chinatown: 1850-1970*. M.A. Thesis, California State University, Northridge, 1973.

◆ McMillan, Penelope. "Los Angeles Chinatown Turns." *Los Angeles Times*, September 18, 1977.

◆ "Old Chinatown." *Los Angeles Herald Examiner*, May 7, 1988.

◆ Ong, Paul, Edna Bonacich, and Lucie Cheng, ed. *The New Asian Immigration in Los Angeles and Global Restructuring*. Philadelphia: Temple University Press, 1994.

◆ Rasmussen, Cecilia. "The City Then and Now." *Los Angeles Times*, August 30, 1993

◆ Redevelopment Project Biennial Report. Los Angeles. Community Redevelopment Agency of the City of Los Angeles, 1986-1988, 1988-1990, 1990-1992, 1997.

◆ Romney, Lee. "Chinese Americans Make Political Strides." *Los Angeles Times*, November. 28, 1993.

◆ Saito, Leland T. "Asian Americans and Latinos in San Gabriel Valley, California: Ethnic Political Cooperation and Redistricting 1990-1992." *Amerasia Journal* 19, no. 2 (1993): 55-68.

◆ Schoenberger, Karl. "Breathing Life into Southland." *Los Angeles Times*, October 4, 1993.

◆ Schoenberger, Karl. "Expatriate entrepreneurs." *Los Angeles Times*, October 3, 1993.

◆ See, Lisa. *On Gold Mountain*. New York: Saint Martin Press, 1995.

◆ Seo, Diane. "Faded Glory." *Los Angeles Times*, November. 1, 1992.

◆ Shaw, David. "New York Times Explains, Critiques Its Lee Coverage." *New York Times*, September 27, 2000.

◆ Sing, Bill. "Chinatown Struggles to Balance Dual Community Roles." *Los Angeles Times*, April 13, 1980.

◆ *The Asian American Almanac*. Gale Research Inc., 1995.

◆ The Chinese Community in Action. *1978 Los Angeles Chinatown Souvenir Book*. Los Angeles: Chinese Chamber of Commerce, 1978.

◆ The Golden Years, 1938-1988. Los Angeles, 1988.

◆ Tom, Kim Fong. *The Participation of the Chinese in the Community Life of Los Angeles*. M.A. Thesis, University of Southern California, 1944.

◆ Tomlinson, John. "Four Lives." *USC Trojan Family Magazine*, Summer 1998.

◆ Tong, Benson. The Chinese Americans. London: Greenwood Press, 2000.

◆ Torres, Vicki. "The Great Wall of Chinatown." *Los Angeles Times*, March 31, 1996.

◆ "Wilbur Woo." *Asian Focus*. November/December 1990.

◆ Wiles, Otis. "War of Great Chinese Tongs." *Los Angeles Times*, January 16, 1921.

◆ Yee, George and Elsie. "The 1927 Chinese Baseball Team." *Gum Saan Journal* (December 1980).

-----------. "The Chinese and the Los Angeles Produce Market." *Gum Saan Journal* (December 1986).

◆ Yee, Mary and Chuck. "The Pioneer Chinese American Actors." *1979 Los Angeles Chinatown Souvenir Book*. Los Angeles: Chinese Chamber of Commerce, 1979.

◆ Yeung, Linda. *Chinatown USA Profile*: The Los Angeles Chapter. Chinatown Service Center, March 25, 1992.

◆ Yung, Judy. *Chinese Women of America: A Pictorial History*. Seattle: University of Washington Press, 1986.

◆ Zasada, Marc Porter. "A Tumultuous History of Chinatown." *Downtown News*, June 6, 1998.

◆ Zazas, James B. *Visions of Luscombe - The Early Years*. 1993.